T0330335

Personnel Management in Secret Service
Organizations

Personnel Management in Secret Service Organizations

Barbara Czarniawska

Professor Emerita of Management Studies, GRI, School of Business, Economics and Law, University of Gothenburg, Sweden

Sabina Siebert

Professor of Management, Adam Smith Business School, University of Glasgow, UK

John Mackay

Literature Tutor, University of Glasgow, UK

 Edward Elgar
PUBLISHING

Cheltenham, UK • Northampton, MA, USA

Published by
Edward Elgar Publishing Limited
The Lypiatts
15 Lansdown Road
Cheltenham
Glos GL50 2JA
UK

Edward Elgar Publishing, Inc.
William Pratt House
9 Dewey Court
Northampton
Massachusetts 01060
USA

A catalogue record for this book
is available from the British Library

Library of Congress Control Number: 2023933597

This book is available electronically in the **Elgar**online
Business subject collection
http://dx.doi.org/10.4337/9781035301256

ISBN 978 1 0353 0124 9 (cased)
ISBN 978 1 0353 0125 6 (eBook)

Printed and bound in Great Britain by TJ Books Limited, Padstow, Cornwall

Contents

Acknowledgments

The study was funded by the British Academy/Leverhulme Small Research Grant "Managing Secret Agents" (SRG1920\101715), for which we are very grateful. Barbara Czarniawska additionally thanks the Foundation for Economic Research in West Sweden for supporting her participation in the project.

List of intelligence officers and agents

Vera Atkins (1908–2000). British intelligence officer. Born in Galati, Romania.
Atkins worked in the France section of the Special Operations Executive (SOE) during the Second World War. After joining the SOE in 1941, she recruited and deployed British agents in occupied France. She was part of the British team that evacuated Poland's Enigma codebreakers across the border into Romania and, ultimately, to Britain. As the intelligence officer of F Section, she attracted controversy after the spy network was breached and 27 agents were killed by the Germans.

George Blake (1922–2020). MI6 spy, worked as double agent for the Soviet Union. Born George Behar in Rotterdam, the Netherlands.
Blake decided to work for the MGB (later to become the KGB), the Soviet state security operation, when he was a prisoner during the Korean War. In 1961, he was sentenced to 42 years in prison, but escaped from Wormwood Scrubs and fled to the Soviet Union. Vladimir Putin said of Blake, "Colonel Blake was a brilliant professional of special vitality and courage."

Anthony Blunt (1907–1983). Spy for the Soviet Union. Born in Bournemouth, England.
Blunt was a leading British art historian, who, in 1964, confessed to having been a spy for the Soviet Union. He was the "Fourth Man" of the Cambridge Five spy ring and during the Second World War passed intelligence on Wehrmacht plans that the British government had decided to withhold from its ally. In his memoirs, Blunt conceded that spying for the Soviet Union was the biggest mistake of his life.

Whittaker Chambers (1901–1961). Spy for the Soviet Union. Born in Philadelphia, USA.
Chambers was a writer-editor who became a member of the Communist Party in 1925 and was a Soviet spy from 1932 to 1938. He then defected from the Soviet underground and worked for *Time* magazine before testifying in the Hiss case for perjury (see Alger Hiss), described as the

trial of the century. Ronald Reagan awarded him the Presidential Medal of Freedom posthumously in 1984.

Eddie Chapman (1914–1997). Double agent—British code name, Zigzag; German code name, Fritz. Born in Burnopfield, County Durham, England.
Chapman was a British double agent during the Second World War. He was code-named Zigzag because of his erratic personal history: before becoming an agent, Chapman was a safecracker for London West End gangs, as a result of which he served several prison sentences. He successfully faked sabotage attacks on the De Havilland aircraft factory in Hatfield, and the ship *The City of Lancaster,* for which he was presented with the Iron Cross in Germany, although the precise nature of this award is disputed.

Eli Cohen (1924–1965). Egyptian-born Israeli spy. Born in Alexandria, Egypt.
From 1961 to 1965, Cohen worked as a spy in Syria, where he developed close relationships with the Syrian political and military hierarchy and became chief adviser to the Minister of Defense. He was hanged at Marjeh Square, Damascus, in 1965 after Syrian counterintelligence uncovered the spy conspiracy. The Netflix series *The Spy* portrays his life.

David Cornwell (1931–2020). Better known as John le Carré. Author and British intelligence officer. Born In Poole, Dorset, England.
Cornwell worked for both MI5 and MI6 during the 1950s and 1960s. For MI6, he worked under the cover of Second Secretary at the British Embassy in Bonn and was later transferred to Hamburg as a political consul, where he wrote *The Spy Who Came in From the Cold* (1963). Le Carré depicted and analyzed Soviet double agent Kim Philby as the mole hunted by George Smiley in *Tinker Tailor Soldier Spy* (1974).

Nicholas (Nick) Elliott (1916–1994). MI6 Intelligence Officer; Head of Station, Secret Intelligence Service in Bern, 1945–53, in Vienna 1953–56, in London 1956–60, in Beirut 1960–62, MI6 director 1963–69. Elliott's career was marked by two notorious events, the death of Commander Lionel Crabb and the flight of double agent Kim Philby to Moscow in 1963.

Juan Pujol García (1912–1988). British agent Garbo; German code name, Alaric. Born in Barcelona, Spain.
Pujol was a double agent loyal to Britain against Germany during the Second World War. He fashioned a fake identity to become a German agent, before moving to Lisbon and creating false reports about Britain from a variety of public sources. Along with his handler Tomás "Tommy" Harris, Pujol expanded his network of fake spies, to the point where Germany was eventually funding a network of 27 agents, all fictitious. Pujol was awarded the Iron Cross in Germany as well as an MBE in Britain.

Michał Goleniewski (1922–1992). Known as Sniper and Lavinia. Born in Nieśwież, Poland, now Belarus.
Goleniewski was a Polish officer in the People's Republic of Poland's Ministry of Public Security. He was the deputy head of military counter-intelligence, later the head of the technical and scientific section of Polish intelligence, and a spy for the Soviet government during the 1950s. In 1959, he became a triple agent, supplying Polish and Soviet secrets to the CIA, which resulted in the exposure of George Blake and Harry Houghton. He defected to the United States in 1961 and, in 1963, started claiming to be Tsarevich Alexei Nikolayevich of Russia.

Filip Hagenbeck (1953–). Also known as Philip (on Facebook) and Filip Bartoszewicz (actual name is probably Wojciech Martynowicz). Born in Warsaw, Poland; studied sociology at Warsaw University.
Between 1979 and 1990, Hagenbeck worked first in Department I (foreign intelligence) and then in Department II (counterintelligence) of the Polish Ministry of Internal Affairs (MIA). In Department II, he was a head of Counterintelligence Branch 10, which was tasked with unmasking foreign spies.

Alger Hiss (1904–1996). Alleged spy for the Soviet Union. Born in Baltimore, USA.
Hiss was a US government official accused of having spied for the Soviet Union in the 1930s. Between 1949 and 1950, former US Communist Party member Whittaker Chambers testified that Hiss had secretly been a communist while in federal service. Hiss served time in prison for perjury but maintained his innocence until his death.

Jane Horney (1918–1945). British citizen but born in Sweden. Swedish and Danish agent.
Horney was thought to have spied in Denmark for Nazi Germany, although the Gestapo believed that she was an agent for Britain or the Soviet Union. In January 1945, Horney was shot, and her body wrapped in chains, before being dropped into the sea. There was dispute over whether the murder happened on Danish or Swedish territory. Some contend that she was not killed at all and died of a heart attack in London in 2003.

Karin Lannby (1916–2007). Swedish actress and spy. Born in Linköping, Sweden.
Lannby served as an agent for the leftists during the Spanish Civil War but failed in her task to infiltrate Franco's troops in the south of France. During the Second World War, she was an agent for Sweden in Stockholm. Under the code name Anette, she supplied details of her observations from the cultural and diplomatic circles of Stockholm's party life. She acted in several films during the war and had a relationship with Ingmar Bergman.

Guy Liddell (1892–1958). British intelligence officer. Born in London, England.
Liddell joined MI5 in 1931 and, in 1940, was promoted to Director of B Division in charge of counterespionage, where he appointed Anthony Blunt to a senior post. Liddell was appointed Deputy Director General of MI5 in 1947. Rumors that he might be a double agent were exacerbated by the defection to Russia of his close friend Guy Burgess, as well as the fact that he was a known associate of Blunt and Kim Philby, other members of the so-called Cambridge Five spy ring. In 1979, he was named as the Fifth Man, but subsequent documents have all but completely cleared him of the charge.

Ashraf Marwan (1944–2007). "The Angel." Diplomat and businessman. Born in Cairo, Egypt.
In the period leading up to the 1973 Arab–Israel War, Marwan was recruited by Egyptian Intelligence and may have fed the Israeli Mossad with misleading information. In Mossad's version, however, he provided Israel with information about the coming war, including Egyptian war plans, accounts of its military exercises, and the documentation of Egypt's arms deals with the Soviet Union and other countries. Thus, the pseudonym "Angel," as the savior of Israel. In 2007, he died in myste-

rious circumstances, apparently falling from the balcony of his London house. His wife accused Mossad of his assassination.

Alexander Orlov (1895–1973). Defector to the United States. Born in Babruysk, Russian Empire (now Belarus).
A colonel in the Soviet secret police, Orlov fled to the United States in 1938 due to fears of execution. Known by numerous code names, Orlov published his memoir, *The Secret History of Stalin's Crimes*, after Stalin's death in 1953.

Oleg Penkovsky (1919–1963). Soviet informer for the United Kingdom; code name, Hero. Born in Vladikavkaz, USSR.
Penkovsky was a Soviet military intelligence colonel during the 1950s and 1960s. He played a crucial role during the Cuban Missile Crisis by providing to the West plans and descriptions of the nuclear rocket launch sites in Cuba. He was one of several individuals credited with altering the course of the Cold War. He was arrested by the Soviets in 1962, then tried and executed the following year.

Kim Philby (1912–1988). British intelligence officer and double agent for the Soviet Union. Born in Ambala, Punjab, British India.
Philby was a member of the Cambridge Five, a spy ring that passed information to the Soviet Union during the Second World War and in the early stages of the Cold War. He tipped off two other spies under suspicion of espionage, Donald Maclean and Guy Burgess, both of whom fled to Moscow in 1951. After being unmasked as a Soviet agent in 1963, he defected to Moscow, where he lived until his death in 1988.

Bruno Pontecorvo (1913–1993). Defector to the Soviet Union. Born in Marina di Pisa, Italy.
Pontecorvo was a nuclear physicist who defected to the Soviet Union in 1950, where he worked at the Joint Institute for Nuclear Research in Dubna. US newspapers discussed his potential role in the transfer of nuclear secrets to Russia, but Pontecorvo never confirmed or denied that he was a spy. After he died, in accordance with his wishes, half of his ashes were buried in Rome and the other half in Dubna, Russia.

Dušan "Dusko" Popov (1912–1981). British and US spy—code name, Tricycle; German code name, Ivan. Born in Titel, Austro-Hungary (present-day Serbia).
Popov was a triple agent who served as part of MI6 and the Abwehr during the Second World War. As part of the double-cross system, he

supplied disinformation to Germany, while also working as an agent (code name Dusko) for the Yugoslav government-in-exile in London. He was code-named Tricycle by MI5 because he oversaw a group of three double agents. In 1944, Popov was a key part of the deception Operation Fortitude, set up to mislead the Germans about the timing, location, and scale of the invasion of Normandy in 1944. He is regarded as one of Ian Fleming's principal inspirations for the character of James Bond.

Stella Rimington (1935–). Director General of MI5, 1992–1996. Born in London, England.
Between 1969 and 1990, Rimington worked in all three branches of the Security Service—counterespionage, countersubversion, and coun terterrorism—before being promoted to Director General in 1992. She was made a Dame Commander of the Order of the Bath in 1996.

Wulf Dietrich Christian Schmidt (1911–1992), known also as Harry Williamson. British code name, Agent Tate; German code name, Leonhardt. Born in Apenrade, Prussia, Germany. Danish citizen.
Schmidt was a double agent working for Britain during the Second World War. He was one of the longest-running agents in the double-cross system, under which all German agents in Britain were controlled by MI5 and deployed to deceive Germany. Schmidt was part of the Operation Bodyguard deception employed by the Allied states before the 1944 invasion of northwest Europe. He was granted naturalization as a German citizen so that he could receive the Iron Cross for his apparent successes.

Vincent V. Severski (1956–). Polish intelligence officer. Real name Włodzimierz Sokołowski. Born in Warsaw, Poland.
Severski served as an intelligence officer for 26 years, almost half of which was outside Poland—he claims to have participated in around 140 operations in almost 50 countries. He was involved in identifying ideological subversion directed at Poland and in investigating the Solidarity trade union, which was established in 1980.

Krystyna Skarbek (1908–1952). Agent of the British Special Operations Executive during the Second World War. Born in Trzepnica, Poland.
Skarbek was celebrated for her daring exploits in intelligence and irregular-warfare missions in Nazi-occupied Poland and France.

Richard Sorge (1895–1944). German journalist and Soviet military intelligence officer. Code name, Ramsay. Born in Baku, Russian Empire, now Azerbaijan.
Sorge served in Japan in 1940 and 1941, when he supplied information about Adolf Hitler's plan to attack the Soviet Union. He was arrested in Japan for espionage and, subsequently, tortured and hanged in 1944. In 1964, he was posthumously awarded the title of Hero of the Soviet Union.

George Tenet (1953–). Director of Central Intelligence for the CIA, 1997–2004. Born in New York City, USA.
Tenet played a principal role in overseeing intelligence regarding weapons of mass destruction before the Iraq War. He was criticized during his tenure at the CIA for authorizing the CIA's use of torture techniques, in contravention of international law. Since 2008 he has been a managing director at investment bank Allen & Company.

Source: Wikipedia

List of secret service organizations

C-bureau: A Swedish secret intelligence agency established in 1939 under the Swedish Armed Forces.

CIA: The Central Intelligence Agency, known informally as "the Agency" and historically as "the Company," is a civilian foreign intelligence service of the federal government of the United States, officially tasked with gathering, processing, and analyzing national security information from around the world.

FBI: The Federal Bureau of Investigation is the domestic intelligence and security service of the United States and its principal federal law enforcement agency. It is the leading US counterterrorism and counterintelligence criminal investigative organization.

FSB: The Federal Security Service of the Russian Federation is Russia's principal security agency and the main successor agency to the Soviet Union's KGB. Its primary responsibilities are within the country and include counterintelligence, internal and border security, counterterrorism, and surveillance, as well as investigation of some other types of serious crimes and federal law violations.

GRU: The Main Directorate of the General Staff of the Armed Forces of the Russian Federation, which, in 1992, took over the activities of the Main Intelligence Directorate, the foreign military intelligence agency of the Soviet Army General Staff of the Soviet Union until 1991.

KGB: The Committee for State Security was the main security agency for the Soviet Union from February 4, 1947, to December 3, 1991.

MIA: This was the Polish Ministry of Internal Affairs (1945–1990) that included Department I (foreign intelligence) and Department II (counterintelligence).

MI5: Military Intelligence, Section 5 (the Security Service), is the United Kingdom's domestic counterintelligence and security agency.

MI6: Military Intelligence, Section 6 (the Secret Intelligence Service, SIS), is the United Kingdom's foreign intelligence service, tasked mainly with the covert overseas collection and analysis of human intelligence in support of the United Kingdom's national security.

Mossad: The national intelligence agency of Israel, it is responsible for intelligence collection, covert operations, and counterterrorism.

SÄPO: The Swedish Security Service is a Swedish government agency organized under the Ministry of Justice. It is responsible for counterespionage and counterterrorism, as well as the protection of dignitaries and the constitution.

SOE: The Special Operations Executive was a secret British Second World War organization, formed in 1940. Its purpose was to conduct espionage, sabotage, and reconnaissance in occupied Europe and to aid local resistance movements.

Stasi: East Germany's State Security Service from 1950 to 1990.

Source: Wikipedia

1. The study

In the project on which this book is based, we studied the work of people employed by secret service organizations, commonly referred to as spies. The term "spy" is, however, a label from popular culture, whereas in practice the employees of secret service organizations are variously referred to as agents, secret agents, undercover agents, intelligence officers, intel analysts—among many other terms, which we present later. In this introduction, we use the word "spy" for the sake of brevity.

We were interested in key events from a spy's career: how they enter their occupation, and how they perform espionage work; how they are trained and managed; and what are the circumstances of their promotion and demotion, up to the point of exit from the profession (through retirement, capture, or death). Our interest stemmed from observation of the crucial but little-known role that secret service organizations— also termed intelligence or espionage agencies—play in societies. For instance, US historian Timothy Snyder (2022) claims in his commentary on the war with Ukraine that Vladimir Putin rebuilt Russia on the model of the KGB, his previous employer.

Fulfilling their regular tasks, secret service organizations gather, scrutinize, and capitalize on information to guard their countries against the political and economic consequences of security violations. The UK Secret Intelligence Service (MI6), the US Central Intelligence Agency (CIA), the Swedish Security Service (SÄPO), and the Russian Federal Security Service (FSB) are some examples of contemporary intelligence organizations. Notable historical agencies include the KGB in the Soviet Union (1954–1991) and East Germany's State Security Service (Stasi, 1950–1990).

Those who were employed as spies tend to cite many different and rather particular motives for joining secret service organizations: ideological persuasion, love of their country, the satisfaction gained from deceiving others, profit seeking, the seduction of danger, and a sense of adventure. Some, but not all, of these reasons may be shared by people employed at what we call "standard" (i.e., non-secret private or public sector) organizations. The significant negative consequences of becoming a spy include discovery, humiliation, deportation, torture, and—in extreme circumstances—death. Of these, one might only experience humiliation in standard organizations, where it is in fact relatively common (Czarniawska, 2008).

We could not rely on conventional research methods in our study because, although the existence of espionage organizations is not secret, their employees' affiliation with espionage is often under wraps. Therefore, although the careers of secret agents have inspired many genres of popular culture (for a review, see, e.g., Boltanski, 2014), relatively little research has been done on spying as an occupation or a profession.

From a legal perspective, it is sometimes forbidden even to acknowledge that something is secret. Nevertheless, there are notable studies of secrecy in first-order secret organizations, as Grey and Costas (2016) called them, such as state security services (see, e.g., Simmel, 1906; Stohl and Stohl, 2011; Grey, 2012); second-order secret organizations, such as intelligence agencies (see, e.g., Parker, 2018; Rombach and Solli, 2019; Walters, 2021); partly secret criminal organizations, such as mafias (Catino, 2019); and non-secret (standard) organizations (Costas and Grey, 2014, 2016). Still, field studies are frequently limited to a historical perspective[1] and conducted at a time when the analysis of declassified information has been allowed (see, e.g., Grey's important study of Bletchley, 2012). As a result, personnel management/Human Resource Management literature contains scant material concerning the management of secret agents and descriptions of their work.

Therefore, we explored conventional aspects of personnel management in these nonconventional organizations, comparing them with knowledge accumulated in studies of personnel management in standard organizations. We believe that the work of secret service agents may prove more relevant to an understanding of managing people in ordinary organizations than is usually assumed (see also Scott, 2013; Costas and Grey, 2016; Parker, 2016). We have also investigated how working under the conditions of secrecy affects professional identities, using investigative devices from narratology to analyze our sources (Czarniawska, 2004).

---

[1]   A "limited perspective" is not necessarily a defect, though. As Grey (2012) pointed out, a historical perspective allows organization scholars to notice what is often taken for granted in studies of contemporary organizations.

We use the term "personnel management" rather than "Human Resource Management" for several reasons. The term "human resources" is controversial: arguably, it reduces people to the same status as materials, buildings, money, and technology. Nevertheless, it is defined by Boxall and Purcell, for example, as "all activities associated with the management of employment relationships in the firm" (2003, p. 1); in their understanding, human resources encompass knowledge, skills, networks, intellectual capabilities, and personalities. Yet, the very word "resources" is somewhat demeaning, and there have been recent attempts to change it, including the coining of such new terms as People Profession (CIPD, 2021), People Operations, or Employee Experience. Thus, although we acknowledge that "personnel management" is an old-fashioned, infrequently used term, we also recognize that a suitable replacement has not been established.

We may add that, at the outset, we treated the title "personnel management" as temporary and somewhat satirical: surely secret service organizations do not consider themselves required to deal with such standard organizational issues? Soon, however, we discovered that, at present, all such known organizations have their own Human Resource Management department. As our research concerns, for obvious reasons, the historical activities of such organizations, we use the traditional name for this management function.

RESEARCH METHODOLOGY

We used two principal types of sources in the study: biographies and autobiographies of spies. Autobiographies of secret agents might be criticized for being fictionalized, but this does not present an obstacle to social scientific analysis. The claim that there is a circular relationship between culture and other fields of social endeavor is not new (see, e.g., Johnson, 1986–1987). Such a "circuit of culture" is especially obvious in the case of popular culture, which transmits ideals and propagates identity models, reflects on actual practices, but also teaches these models to practitioners (Czarniawska and Rhodes, 2006). In addition, it offers interpretative templates, patterns for sensemaking. This connection, as noted by Boltanski (2014), is especially evident in the case of spy fiction and spy diaries. Societal perception of this profession is almost entirely based on these two kinds of sources, due to the lack of field studies and the length of time required for declassification.

Nevertheless, the use of autobiographies and biographies is not exclusive to spy studies; however, they are rarely used as field material in organization studies, and as such they may need a more thorough introduction. As Laura Marcus observed, "The term 'autobiography' (...) breaks down into its component parts—'auto' (self), 'bios' (life), 'graphein' (writing). The element of writing or text is inscribed in the term itself. Language, as well as the workings of memory, shapes the past" (2018, p. 2).

This definition raises questions about the nature of the "self," about what constitutes a "life," and how writing might be used to construct a life after the event. The "workings of memory" are notoriously unreliable and prone to embellishment through the medium of "language"—whether that language is deployed autobiographically by the spy or, alternatively, by a biographer, the disconnected agent of a life's reconstruction.

Language will always represent rather than recreate the subjects in their fullness, and in any case, language can only ever describe a fragment of what constitutes the Other. The singular Other remains in a place that is beyond language—there will always be the untranslated portion, the surplus that is beyond reach. Given that there will always be a part of the subject that remains uncaptured and unarticulated, how does the biographer decide which fragments to retrieve? The very nature of an archival fragment—decontextualized and potentially incoherent—means that the biographer remains at risk of an inadequate representation of the subject. In these circumstances, how can the reader begin to work at developing a conception of the subject? This question acquires particular importance when the readers are researchers with analytical goals, and the subjects were working as spies.

There is an unavoidable tension for the biographer when comparing spies' private incarnations—shrouded in mystery—and their public representations. After all, the intense secrecy and layers of deception that constitute an intelligence agent's life are irredeemably exposed when a biography enters the world. A life that was conducted under a cloak of bluff and double bluff now becomes part of a public conversation, a strand in the fabric of cultural discourse. This dramatic shift is even more obvious in the case of autobiographies. Not only the self, but also the driving dynamic of a spy's life become fashioned in the resulting text because "...autobiography (like the novel) involves not only the construction of self, but also a construction of one's culture" (Bruner, 2001, p. 35). In this task, biographers are aided by the archives, but even this stage of the process is not without its complications.

The notion of secrecy is central to the culture of a spy's life and work, a trait that is replicated in the archive itself. It is a space in which the tension between concealment (the essence of spy work) and revelation (that which is desired by the reader) plays out. The multiple layers of secrecy pertaining to spies and their activities are reinforced, and overlaid, by the integral secrecy of the archive, with its various lacunae and fragments.

Yet, the very idea of writing a biography, understood as excavating a site of information and probing beneath surfaces, has a strong resonance with the work of a spy. The work of the biographer is inevitably a contentious exercise—both in terms of selecting material for inclusion and the ways in which such material is handled. As Backscheider observed, "Evidence—finding it, evaluating it, presenting it—is the greatest test of the biographer" (1999, p. xiii).

The distinction between what is seen and unseen—not only by enemy forces, but also by the reader—serves as a reminder that archival work can never be entirely impartial. Biographers' work is subject to scrutiny regarding the material they selected for inclusion and the way in which they chose to configure the textual fragments of the subject. Regardless of any personal connection that might have been enjoyed by the biographer during the lifetime of the subject, the biography remains an imagined retrieval of an imagined Other. The voice of the subject is always to some extent filtered through the agency of the biographer.

> Any portrait of another human being ... will require an element of fiction beyond that afforded by the written record. And during the writing, adherence to the real, the actual, is gradually augmented by adherence to the imagined, the inferred, the supposed, to your educated but imperfect impression of what this or that person was like. (Jensen, 2022)

Archives lure biographers with the promise of enabling them to tread the ground the former spy occupied, but the "omissions, restrictions, repressions, and exclusions" (Collis, 2006, p. 19) of this territory serve to foreground precisely what cannot be recovered.

There is also what we might term the hybrid publication, where a spy "autobiography" is co-authored by a professional writer. In the Introduction to Volume 1 of *The Guy Liddell Diaries*, editor Nigel West claimed to have shed light on some "events that hitherto have been shrouded in an almost comprehensive cloak of official secrecy," adding that "not a single MI5 officer ever published an account of his war work, and those who sought permission to do so were discouraged and even threatened. A very few wartime officers were allowed to make veiled references to their temporary employment by the Security Service..." (2005a, p. 3). Would Liddell have been able to bring those "events" to life without West's help? From Macintyre's biography of Eddie Chapman, known as Agent Zigzag, readers learn that "Eddie Chapman's memoirs were published after the war, but the Official Secrets Act prevented him from describing his exploits as a double agent, and his own version of events was often more entertaining than reliable" (2007, p. 320).

García and West also noticed the "wall of secrecy" that shielded Juan Pujol García, known as Garbo, the Spanish spy who served as a double agent loyal to Great Britain against Nazi Germany during the Second World War:

> GARBO's extraordinary contribution to the Allied victory is well documented. There is hardly a textbook on the subject of strategic deception that fails to mention this remarkable individual. But no author has ever succeeded in penetrating the wall of secrecy that MI5, the British Security Service, constructed around their star performer. His true identity remained as closely guarded in 1984 as it was at the end of the war, when elaborate arrangements were made to protect him for the rest of his life. (2011, p. 5)

The cloak of silence that descends on spies and settles around their activities while they are still living and working continues after their death. Carmen Maria Machado reflected on the nature of the archive and, in particular, on the concept of "archival silence," which "illustrates a difficult truth: sometimes stories are destroyed, and sometimes they are never uttered in the first place; either way something very large is irrevocably missing from our collective histories" (2019, p. 2).

Archival material often consists of fragments, incoherent shards; in the case of information that relates to spies, it is further fractured by censorship and put in doubt by questions regarding its reliability. The biographer might be enticed into approaching the spy, only to find, as García and West discovered, that "the conundrum remains as insoluble as ever" (2011, p. 198). In this respect, the unreliability of the narrator adds a frustrating level of complexity and depth to any conundrum that exists for the biographer. In Volume 2 of his diaries, Liddell (West, 2005b) observed that what is most frustrating for the controller of a spy—the lack of accuracy in the reports—may be most appealing to the reader. In effect, readers may be less interested in accuracy and more in whether the narrative lives up to expectations related to the genre. Thus, both the former spy writing their autobiography and the biographer attempting to encapsulate the former spy may respond to inherent pressures to spice up particular aspects of the spy's life. As a result, passages become susceptible to exaggeration and embellishment, or plain untruth. It is, therefore, likely that quite a proportion of the readership of (auto)biographies will have what Boltanski termed "a selfish way of looking which is wholly taken up with the internal states aroused by the spectacle... fascination, horror, interest, excitement, pleasure" (1999, p. 21). Such readers may demand from the (auto)biography a satisfying emotional experience, rather like the thrill that might be experienced by watching 007 on the big screen. However, "spying is a grubby, sordid business. As fiction readers and cinema goers we have (...) been misled into expecting espionage stories to bear at least some resemblance to the tropes of a Bond movie: fast cars, beautiful women, heroic derring-do and monochromatically wicked villains" (Tate, 2021, loc. 6127).

Such sexed-up material may titillate many readers, but it might prove obfuscatory for researchers aiming at an analysis of the substance of the text. In this respect, the author of a spy (auto)biography may find themselves juggling a desire for excitement with the demand for accuracy—not an easy requirement to fulfill. Bruner asserted that

> ... an autobiography is not and cannot be a way of simply signifying or referring to a "life as lived"... a life is created or constructed by the art of autobiography. It is a way of construing experience—and of reconstruing and reconstruing it until our breath or our pen fails us. Construal and reconstrual are interpretive. (1995, p. 161)

As any agent might admit if pressed for a strictly truthful account of events, the life of a spy is not solely composed of daring, romantic feats of bravery. Rather, it is a narrative, which, somewhat like the spy, crosses various borders into the realms of opacity, secrecy, and fiction. "Any narrative of the self and its life-story will entail a reconstruction, subject to the vagaries of memory, which renders the division between autobiography and fiction far from absolute" (Marcus, 2018, p. 4).
Or, as Brockmeier pointed out,

> The problem of authenticity arises. To create the impression of first-hand authenticity and to make the story convincing is what all autobiographical narratives are about. Yet there is probably no first-person life story that would not sooner or later encounter the question of how authentic, how "real" it is. (2001, pp. 266–267)

Again, waters become further muddied in the case of spies' (auto)biographies. A spy is employed to engage in deception—effectively, to lie for a living. The autobiographical genre does not confer any guarantee of genuineness on the words that issue from the writer. The autobiographical text is constructed by events that have taken place outside the author and is articulated via language that is channeled through others.

According to Denise Riley, material for the autobiography arrives from sources outside the self: "My autobiography always arrives from somewhere outside me; my narrating I is really anybody's, promiscuously" (2000, p. 58). What constitutes the self is so slippery and multivalent that it has the potential to instill the autobiographical text with a deep unease. Riley noted "the awkwardness stubbornly attached to using the first person" (2000, p. 59).

Stir into this cocktail the multivalent layering of a spy's life—of an individual who is well drilled in the essential practice of fashioning a multiplicity of selves—and the (auto)biographical text is vulnerable to much uncertainty. As Laura Marcus observed,

> Complex understandings of the nature of self and identity, influenced by early 20th-century philosophies and by psychoanalysis, led to the view that conventional forms of autobiography were not adequate to the multiplicity of selves that make up the single individual. The self was understood to have substrates which were not knowable and communicable in any direct way. Autobiographical fiction, with its possibilities for multiple perspectives on characters and situations, answered to the need to represent complex, composite, and divided selves, creating the most appropriate vehicles for identities which can never be fully known. (2018, p. 112)

An additional problem regarding the scrutiny of spies' (auto)biographies is that their composite selves also included their "legends," cover stories that could sound more authentic than real-life accounts. As Miller puts it:

> Thousands of pages of documents lodged in the National Archives in Washington and London chronicle [Dušan] Popov's [triple agent Tricycle] astonishing career, although they are a minefield for the unwary researcher. One afternoon at the Public Records Office in Kew I was reading a long and extraordinarily detailed report about how Popov had met an Indian technician in New York, who had agreed to build a radio transmitter for him—only to discover, belatedly, that the whole story had been dreamed up by British intelligence as part of Popov's cover. None of it was true. (2004, loc. 62–82)

It is evident that any (auto)biographical subject—regardless of whether they are a spy—cannot be compressed into a single, unadulterated self. Any life is also subject to the capricious nature of memory. The assertions made in a memoir—nonfiction narrative writing based on the author's personal memories—may be understood to be factual, but are they accurate?

> At its most superficial–definitional, a memoir is a recounting of memories. A writer may (as many writers have) undertake a memoir for purposes of saving his/her past from oblivion (seemingly), believing the textual version to be as legitimate as the original experience of events, buying into a mindset that the memories on which the text is based are uncomplicatedly accurate, never considering the subtle (or great) differences of shaped perspective or later molding. In other words, "straight" memoir presents itself as if there were a direct and transparent relation among act and memory and text. (Madden, 2014, p. 229)

The incessant scheming that lies at the heart of a spy's life echoes the codification that eventually brings a version of that life to the page. As Jerome Bruner put it:

> The theories or stories one constructs about one's growth and, indeed, about the "stages" along the path of that growth are not verifiable in the usual sense that that term is used. The best one can do is to check them against one's own memory—which, of course, is notoriously fallible and open to schematization. (2001, p. 28)

Thus warned by literary theorists, we read spies' (auto)biographies while keeping firmly in mind Bruner's warning that an autobiography is "a account of what one thinks one did in what settings in what ways for what felt reasons" (1990, p. 119).

Our analysis was conducted taking into consideration the cultural and temporal context within which secret service agents worked, and we analyzed biographies and autobiographies mostly based in the contexts with which we are familiar—Western, Northern, Central, and Eastern Europe, with shorter excursions to Israel and the United States. We read relevant sources in English, Italian, Polish, Russian, and Swedish. When relevant, we also intend to introduce a historical dimension comparing the work of spies in different periods of time, starting from the First World War up to the present, though recent materials are scarce, for obvious reasons.

VOCABULARY AND CATEGORIES USED

Intelligence workers have different labels in different countries and different languages. This is why we needed to introduce a common vocabulary for use in this text, and to which we shall translate labels used in various sources. "Intelligence officers" are employed by intelligence-collecting organizations—the military or police, for instance—though they can also be formally employed by other organizations—diplomatic, for example. Intelligence officers collect information themselves, but they also recruit and run "agents"—who collect information and are being paid, in one way or another, but are not formally employed by a secret organization. There are also "information contacts" (joes, Ics), who provide information for various reasons— because they want to or because they are being blackmailed, for instance—sometimes not even knowing that they are providing it to intelligence officers (Hagenbeck, 2019). All these differentiations apply also to "counterintelligence officers," or "spycatchers."

The term "recruitment" is used—in the practice of intelligence and in this text—in two different contexts: (1) the recruitment of intelligence officers, more or less following the usual practices of organizational recruitment, and (2) the recruitment of agents, an important operation performed by intelligence officers. Also, line management is practiced at different levels, just like in standard organizations. In the vocabulary of intelligence, however, officers are supervised or monitored by their "controllers"; agents are "run" by their "spymasters" or "spymistresses." Agents who spy on their own country of origin are called "agents-in-place" (Tate, 2021). Sleeper spies are placed in a target country or organization and are not supposed to undertake immediate tasks, but to act as a potential asset if activated.

We divided our material into personnel management functions, whose literature we have also used in our analysis. Some changes were needed to fit this special subject, so we used the following list as a framework, where the main points are also the titles of our chapters:

- Getting selected
    - Selection criteria (deduced from the traits of persons selected, as described in biographies and autobiographies)

- Recruitment processes
    - Designing the recruitment strategy, composing a job description, advertising

- Evaluating potential candidates by means of interviews, assessment procedures, reference collection, security vetting (in a standard organization, this is a part of selection that comes after candidates have expressed interest in the job; in secret service organizations, it is mostly the other way round)

- The Office
  - Organization of the office
  - Profiling (legends)
  - Stationing agents/officers in the field

- Training
  - Teaching specific skills
  - Exercising for fitness, health, and safety
  - Team working
  - Testing

- Line management
  - Task allocation
  - Communication with subordinates
  - Communication with upper echelons
  - Managing operations
  - Performance management (assessment and feedback)

- Rewards and sanctions
  - Rewards
  - Sanctions
  - Lack of rewards or sanctions

- Termination
  - Voluntary separation (retirement, change of employment)
  - Involuntary separation (death in service, compulsory retirement, dismissal)

- Personnel management in secret service organizations (compared with standard organizations)
  - Is spying a profession?
  - How far have secret organizations gone on their professionalization route?

2.   Getting selected

What the hell do you think spies are? [asks Alec Leamas, the British spy who
was shot on the Berlin Wall, sacrificed for an ex-Nazi turned Communist who
was a British mole] They're just a bunch of seedy, squalid bastards like me:
little men, drunkards, queers, hen-pecked husbands, civil servants playing
cowboys and Indians to brighten their rotten little lives.
(*The Spy Who Came in from the Cold*, 1965 screenplay, based on the novel by
John le Carré)

In standard organizations, selection is a part of the recruitment process
performed after a "pool" of candidates has been assembled, whereas
in secret organizations, selection seems to precede recruitment. This is
one reason for separating the activities of selection from the recruitment
processes in the present text; also, because it is impossible to establish
with any certainty what intentions the recruiters had when selecting their
targets. Recruitment processes can be described from many sources,
while selection criteria have been deduced from the biographies we
studied: what kind of people became spies?

Obviously, there wasn't one homogeneous group. In this chapter, we
divided our analysis into time periods, but there were many different
dimensions within each of those periods. Spies worked for different
countries (although here one can see more similarities than distinctions,
as intelligence organizations imitated each other), and the roles of individual spies varied. There were discrete requirements for intelligence
officers working in the office, for agents-in-place, and for informers, as
there were, at least partly, for men and women.

1919–1938

The Soviets

Richard Sorge, the German who was an agent working for the Soviet-led Comintern[1] (before it was closed by Stalin and before Sorge was arrested) in Japan, could be seen as the archetype of a spy working in the field. This is how he was described by his biographer:

> Sorge was both an idealistic communist and a cynical liar. He saw himself as a soldier of the revolution, a member of an exalted class of secret party cadres entrusted with the sacred task of penetrating the citadels of the USSR's imperialist enemies. But at the same time he was a pedant, a drunk, and a womaniser. He was addicted to risk, a braggart, often wildly undisciplined. On his frequent alcoholic binges, he crashed cars and motorcycles, drunkenly confessed his love for Stalin and the Soviet Union to audiences of Nazis, and recklessly seduced the wives of his most valuable agents and closest colleagues. (Matthews, 2019, loc. 92)

Many spies drank too much and many, like Sorge, were serial seducers (indeed, Sorge's facility for putting people at ease was almost magical). But what Matthews emphasized in his description of Sorge was something he called "a profound compulsion to deceive," which he compared to an addiction (2019, loc. 100).

Matthews emphasized Sorge's paradoxical character, of which Sorge himself did not seem to be aware. As a communist, he regarded himself a champion of the workers, which did not prevent him from being an intellectual snob. Also, his job required him to play the debauched bourgeois, spending much of his time in the casinos, brothels, and dance halls of prewar Shanghai and Tokyo, which apparently left him largely untroubled.

He was sometimes suspected of being a double agent, which, in a sense, was correct: he provided the Germans with information about Japan, as long as it was not against Soviet interests. As Matthews pointed out, he was possibly the only person in history who was a member of both the German Nazi Party and the Soviet Communist Party. Matthews compared him to Whittaker Chambers, a US communist who also became a Soviet spy, in that they were both "mesmerised by the secret

---

[1] Communist International (1919–1943) was an international organization propagating world communism; it was located in, and run by, the Soviet Union.

world's mixture of bloody ruthlessness and high ideals" (2019, loc. 1023). Also, and of interest in our analysis, British double agent Kim Philby and Sorge, though of different generations and nationalities, were very similar in that they both found "normal life" dull—they needed something more (Matthews, 2019).

1939–1954

MI5 and MI6, United Kingdom

Intelligence officers working in the MI5 office were usually good at languages and had analytical skills. Here is a description of George Leggett, David Cornwell's (le Carré) senior officer, but also his friend:

> The son of an English father and a Polish mother, Leggett had read modern languages at Cambridge during the war; he spoke Russian as well as French, German and Polish. While still in his early twenties he had served as an interpreter at the Potsdam Conference (…). Afterwards he had been recruited into MI5, where he had proved himself to be an analyst of outstanding quality. (Sisman, 2015, p. 127)

Stella Rimington, who in 1992 became MI5's first woman Director General, so described its employees:

> There were no Jews among the 150-odd MI5 officers, and certainly no black faces to be seen in Leconfield House. Nor were there many women in senior positions: one of the few was the fiercely loyal and hardworking Milicent Bagot, the Service's expert on international Communism, who had been with MI5 since 1931, the first woman within the Service to reach the rank of assistant director. (…) Younger officers were wary of her as a stickler for meticulous office procedure; moreover, she was a difficult colleague, whose robust opinions were expressed with passionate conviction. But her memory for facts was so extraordinary as to have passed into Service folklore (…). (Sisman, 2015, p. 190)

And this from Cornwell (le Carré):

> Most of these men were recruited in middle age; with no promise of a career progression, they lacked motivation or drive to exert themselves; many were merely serving out their time until they could collect their pensions. (…) For MI5 officers, a sense of humour was regarded as indispensable, both for preserving a sense of proportion when dealing with issues of national security and for maintaining team spirit. The prevalent atmosphere when David joined

seems to have been informal, jolly, almost schoolboyish. (Sisman, 2015, p. 191)

As for those who were selected to be recruited, Cornwell remarked in his autobiography:

> You had to have gone to a good school, preferably a private one, and to a university, preferably Oxbridge. Ideally, there should already be spies in your family background, or at least a soldier or two. Failing that, at some point unknown to you, you had to catch the eye of a headmaster, tutor or dean who, having judged you a suitable candidate for recruitment, summoned you to his rooms, closed the door and offered you a glass of sherry and an opportunity to meet interesting friends in London. (le Carré, 2016, p. 164)

As we will show later, "the English spy," true or imagined, seemed to be a model imitated in other countries. However, it is likely that this image was somewhat idealized—as illustrated by Nicholas Elliott, an MI6 intelligence officer and a friend of Philby. Apparently, he was recruited more or less by chance, but was judged to have the correct external characteristics for the job. Macintyre described this state of affairs as follows:

> Nicholas Elliott was not obviously cut out to be a spy. His academic record was undistinguished. He knew little about the complexities of international politics, let alone the dexterous and dangerous game being played by MI6 in the run-up to war. Indeed, he knew nothing whatsoever about espionage, but he thought spying sounded exciting, and important, and exclusive. Elliott was self-confident as only a well-bred, well-heeled young Etonian, newly graduated from Cambridge, with all the right social connections, can be. He was born to rule (though he would never have expressed that belief so indelicately) and membership of the most selective club in Britain seemed like a good place to start doing so. (2014, p. 3)

SOE, United Kingdom

The SOE (Special Operations Executive), started in 1940, employed several women, including a "spymistress," as Vera Atkins was known (Stevenson, 2011). Some of these women were responsible for dealing with coded messages, which required a certain skill set.

> The question asked of each bright young female interviewed to handle coded traffic was "Are you good at crossword puzzles?" To answer "Not really" could be decisive. Did she love music? A negative was just as bad. "Terrible at arithmetic?" A despairing and reluctant "Yes" was greeted with a smile that

astonished the candidate. Vera knew any damage done by a math teacher at school was easily repaired, but if the puzzled woman had a tin ear and disliked crossword puzzles, she was shunted into some other service. (Stevenson, 2011, p. 209)

But there were also women agents working in the field, including the Polish Countess Krystyna Skarbek.

Krystyna Skarbek was born in May 1915 on a large family estate outside Warsaw. She had been a rebel at school. "It was Catholic, and I had a Jewish mother," Krystyna said later. "That was as bad as having divorced parents. I was stigmatized as 'unruly' after I set fire to a nun." She regularly climbed mountains as a youngster, got to know all the ski instructors at the winter resort of Zakopane, and smuggled cigarettes, tobacco, and Polish vodka across the frontier for fun. The experience was proving more useful now than good marks. (Stevenson, 2011, p. 161)

Working-class women, such as Violetta Szabo, were also welcome. The primary quality required of SOE agents was a good knowledge of the country in which they were to operate and, especially, its language. Dual nationality was highly appreciated, except in a neutral country such as Sweden, where it could be a burden, arousing suspicions regarding which country the person was loyal to (Bergman, 2014).

C-bureau, Sweden

C-bureau was a Swedish secret intelligence agency established in 1939 under the Swedish Armed Forces. One of its bosses, Helmuth Ternberg, checked the suitability of young women to become agents by pretending to court them (Bergman, 2014). He looked for women sharing similar life histories. They didn't come from the same social background: some of the women were from the countryside, others from Stockholm; some were working class, others middle class; one was a daughter of a director of film company, another the child of a high-level officer. According to Bergman, the women Ternberg selected had certain things in common: they may have been raped as children; their fathers tended to be brutal, often absent; their mothers cold and unreliable.

These women saw themselves as "modern": they drank, smoked, went to nightclubs, and used men they encountered for their own purposes. Yet, according to Bergman, all those Ternberg selected dreamed of meeting a "Prince Charming" and then living a "normal life," filled with love and respect. "It was this duplicity that made them perfect to be used by the military secret service. All security and secret services love young women with this kind of a past, and especially if they work as a secretary to the right person. These were the criteria that Ternberg used" (Bergman, 2014, p. 136).[2]

Another recruit was Jane Horney, a Swedish–Dane who married Herje Granberg, the Berlin correspondent for a Swedish newspaper. The couple divorced in 1943, and Horney moved back to Sweden, where she became one of Ternberg's women.

> Jane Horney was a fantastic recruit. She could with no effort move in very different circles, had a very wide contact network, despite her young age; she was pretty, open and extrovert. She soon learned how to fit very different social occasions. During her stay in Berlin, she accumulated many friends, acquaintances, and contacts that she could exploit later. Jane Horney had a special influence on men—many fell in love with her, and she had several relationships.
>
> She was very different from Ternberg's other girls. She needed no training; she was a natural talent! (Bergman, 2014, p. 25)

Another famous female agent was Karin Lannby, later called "the Swedish Mata Hari" (Guillou, 2019/2020). Lannby spoke eight or nine languages and wrote excellent long reports on a typewriter; she was able to sit through a long party, and then come home and write everything down.

> Karin Lannby was extremely good at playing various social roles, unmatched in making contacts, in reading people, and figuring out which persons were important. She was also a talented linguist, and her bourgeois upbringing had taught her how to behave in fine society. In addition, she had an extensive and practical knowledge of politics and extremist movements, and a direct experience of intelligence work. She was simply the perfect agent... (Bergman, 2014, p. 200)

---

[2] Translations from Swedish B.C.

Of course, Ternberg also selected and recruited male agents, following "the English criteria for a perfect spy."

> He was educated in the school for officers and has very good certificates—in all subjects except for discipline; there he got lots of critique.
> — Is it good for a spy, not to be disciplined?
> — For us it is very good. He decides himself. He is what Americans call an "entrepreneur," "know-how-to-fix-it," an unconventional and result-oriented Jesuit, undoubtedly dangerous in peace time, indispensable in war. (…)

> He grew up learning the ideals of a German–Baltic family, surrounded by women, so he is exceptionally good with them.... He is a real womanizer—a woman that will not be charmed by him has not yet been born. He is the archetype of an international adventurer, in a positive sense. Also, his looks talk for him (…) he is a splendid Aryan—tall, blond, and well-built. Germans must be loving him just for his perfect looks! He is urbane and shows all the signs of a well-educated officer: kisses ladies' hands… is assertive … has a positive attitude and has a contagious smile (Bergman, 2014, pp. 58–59).

Double Agents

United Kingdom–Soviet Union
Apparently, "the characteristics that the KGB recruiter Arnold Deutsch had identified in Philby, Maclean and others, and had listed as attributes of a successful spy [were] an inherent class resentfulness, a predilection for secretiveness and a yearning to belong" (Sisman, 2015, p. 134).

Germany–United Kingdom
Eddie Chapman (Zigzag), who worked for the Germans and the British, was even more peculiar than Sorge; among other reasons, because he lacked any ideological involvement.

> Even by the standards of the fantasists, putative playboys and incompetents who tried to spy against the Allies during that war, Eddie Chapman was unique. An ex-guardsman, a fiercely proud Geordie and, at various times, a petty criminal, a film extra, a wrestler, a self-confessed habitué of the Soho nightlife—indeed, later a nightclub owner—he had already achieved noto-riety before the war as a safebreaker. Serving time in a Jersey jail when the Germans invaded, Eddie had offered to work for the enemy as a saboteur and spy. His offer had been received with alacrity. (Booth, 2007, loc. 152)

And from the German perspective:

> In the early days, the Abwehr chose men who were loyal to the Fatherland by birth, preferring businessmen who went on regular travels around the world. They later began to select people who could be put under pressure. (…) When the details of an Englishman with a criminal record emerged, small wonder that officers in the Abwehr took a great deal of interest. (Booth, 2007, loc. 1459)

Harry Williamson (Tate), born Wulf Schmidt in Germany, was another double agent working for the same countries.

> There were three criteria that should be fulfilled before MI5 could consider someone as a potential recruited double agent, besides, of course, being able to trust the person. The arrest of the person should have occurred quickly after arrival, the agent should not have had time to communicate with the Germans, and the arrest should have taken place without public knowledge. Wulf Schmidt fitted these requirements and was rapidly recruited as a double agent. (Jonason and Olsson, 2011, p. 30)

An interesting question, of course, is how MI5 decided that a person could be trusted (especially considering the idiosyncrasies of many agents). With time, the developing technologies—such as lie detectors—made judgments easier, but not always correct.

1955–1976

Mossad, Israel

We came across the biographies of two Egyptians who worked for Mossad. The first, Eli Cohen (1924–1965), offered his services to Mossad twice, but was rebuked. A Military Intelligence evaluation of some years earlier concluded

> … that Cohen had a high IQ, great bravery, a phenomenal memory, and the ability to keep a secret; but the tests also showed that "in spite of his modest appearance, he has an exaggerated sense of self-importance," and "a lot of internal tension." Cohen, the results indicated, "does not always evaluate danger correctly, and is liable to assume risks beyond those which are necessary." (Jewish Virtual Library, 2007)

Mossad had a policy of not accepting volunteers as field agents, fearing that they may be simple adventurers; yet, by 1960, when the border with

Syria was heating up, they were ready to take another look at Cohen. He was born in Egypt, had oriental features, was known to be selfless and fearless in pursuit of a cause, and spoke Arabic, English, and French. They also knew that he was daring, of superior intelligence, and possessed an exceptional memory (Spier, 2015).

Ashraf Marwan (known as "the Angel," as he had allegedly saved Israel from the Arabs in the war of 1973) offered his services to Mossad and was treated with a certain suspicion, but his vicinity to two Egyptian Presidents (being a son-in-law of Nasser and an adviser to Sadat) prevailed. According to his biographer, Bar-Joseph, he offered his services to the Israeli intelligence service for two principal reasons. One was money, which could provide him with his desired lifestyle, and the other was his yearning for power. "His narcissism expressed itself in an infinite craving for honor, power and influence, and the insistence that people follow his advice" (2017, p. 29).

As for women working for Mossad, allegedly they have only recently been permitted to speak about their work and lives, but they were clearly valued for their special talents: "Their brains invent daring and ingenious operations that make the difference between success and failure. They bring to bear a capacity to improvise, rare expertise, sophisticated weaponry, command of languages, and psychological insight. They have to get inside the mind of the other."[3]

1977–1989

Ministry of Internal Affairs, Poland

Vincent Severski (a pseudonym of Włodzimierz Sokołowski) was a Polish spy during the Cold War and ended his work for the intelligence service in 1989. Here are fragments of an interview conducted by a journalist from the weekly *Polityka* on June 28, 2011:

> I: Why do people join intelligence?
> S: Motivations differ. Those who go for money crumble out fastest. I worked to a large extent for adventure, and later by a habit, but also with a sense of responsibility for the homeland. After years of work, you simply no longer

---

[3]   https://en.globes.co.il/en/article-1000786218, accessed July 19, 2021.

know another life, another world. Constantly elevated adrenaline, a sense of incredible adventure that accompanies all this, it draws you in (...).
I: What features are most desirable in intelligence work?
S: I focused on eccentrics, on unconventional persons. Although they cause problems, they often have unique skills or knowledge in a given field. To be a good operational and reconnaissance officer, you must be able to manipulate the human psyche, to play. But you can't be an actor. I know a few actors who worked in our company, they were completely unsuitable for this profession. We mainly work with our heads (...).
The ability to manipulate is a powerful weapon because you know how to mess up people's minds, you can manipulate them so that they do what you want, follow your instructions, and they often must make dramatic decisions[4].

Severski also emphasized in this interview that despite, or perhaps because of, the extreme sociality required from agents, they are very lonely: "Living in intelligence is very similar to living in a religious order—a closed world, rules, interactions based on trust" (ibid.).

SO, WHO WERE "THE TYPICAL SPIES"?

As John le Carré observed, spies make for tremendously unreliable narrators because they have so often invented and reinvented themselves. (Matthews, 2019, loc. 162)

Bar-Joseph, also suspicious of spies' self-descriptions, offered a review of research aimed at establishing the traits typical for (at least famous) spies. Not all his conclusions, however, were exactly in tune with his own description of Marwan and with those that we could draw. He listed five main motives—"ideology, money, ego, extortion and sexual temptation" (2017, p. 27)—as well as that "of dual loyalty with a country of origin or strong ethnic affiliation" (ibid.). He summed it up as follows:

By itself (...) greed is rarely enough of a motive to undertake something so morally problematic and personally dangerous as betraying one's country. Studies have suggested that such behavior is connected to specific personality patterns. One of the most striking is the tendency to divide one's loyalties, including an inclination to extramarital affairs. Another is a tendency toward narcissism and egocentrism—often expressed in a dysfunctional relationship with one's employer or spouse, and a sense of being unappreciated in their talents and achievements. Further studies, covering cases of deserters and

---

[4]   https://www.polityka.pl/tygodnikpolityka/kraj/1517024,1,rozmowa-z -bylym-agentem-polskiego-wywiadu.read, accessed June 28, 2011, transl. BC.

traitors during the Cold War, have noted that many suffered from the untimely loss of, or a problematic relationship with, their fathers. The sense of loss, these studies suggest, is channeled into action and motivation to offer their service to the enemy. (2017, pp. 28–29)

The problem with this explanation is that, much as this psychological description of spies is correct (the so-called father factor has been mentioned in relation to women agents as well), there are many people who fit this description, but do not become spies.

In our view, spy selection functioned in quite a similar way across time periods and countries. As far as the intelligence officers were concerned, analytical skills were needed, but they were sometimes judged simply on the basis of the elite schools they attended, or even—in the case of women—on their ability to crack a crossword clue.

Agents in the field shared psychological traits: the need for an adrenaline rush (boring lives were frowned upon) and a talent for deception (even an "addiction," as it was called in the case of Richard Sorge) in tandem with seduction skills (for both men and women). Recently, sociologists and organization scholars have begun to pay more attention to what is called "erotic capital" (Hakim, 2010; Abubakar et al., 2019; Syper-Jędrzejak, 2020). Swedish sociologist Hans L. Zetterberg (1969/2002) paid attention to a particularly visible characteristic in spy biographies—what Catherine Hakim (2010, p. 502) called "a probability of being able to induce a state of emotional surrender in persons of the opposite sex" (the second element in Hakim's list of six).

Another noticeable aspect of spies' personalities was a craving for both power and money. They were fond of an active social life, effortlessly making other people feel at ease, which was coupled with a preference for expensive evening entertainment. In most cases, they showed a high tolerance for alcohol. In sharp contrast with the culture of standard organizations, where sanctions would have been enforced, the accounts we analyzed contain numerous references to bars and licensed restaurants on the actual premises of espionage agencies. However, most spies' performance did not appear to be affected by their heavy drinking. Ben Macintyre, one of Kim Philby's biographers, concluded that no one served (or consumed) alcohol with quite the same joie de vivre and determination as Philby. He was a formidable drinker, but he was not alone. Drinking was believed to relieve stress.

> Even by the heavy-drinking standards of wartime, the spies were spectacular boozers. Alcohol helped to blunt the stress of clandestine war, serving as both a lubricant and a bond, and the gentlemen's clubs were able to obtain supplies for their members far beyond the reach of ordinary rationed folk. (Macintyre, 2014, p. 24)

In addition, spies were undoubtedly very intelligent, and a good memory was crucial in their job. It seems that most spies shared the attitude that, in Philby's times, was called "exceptionalism" (Hanning, 2021, p. 144) and that has since become more commonly known as "narcissism" (p. 348).

As for informants, they were sometimes acting in response to a threat; they were often in need of money, and they may have been inspired by ideology. While both agents and informants often claimed an ideological belonging, it is hard to say to what degree it was just the necessary element of a legend and to what extent a genuine belief. Most likely, even the spies themselves didn't know.

Hanning interviewed Stephen Dorril, an authority on MI6, who suggested an interesting explanation for the behavior of successful spies:

> Philby is not unique among MI6 officers in seemingly having what appears to be two personalities. (...) There is a neglected psychological idea—doubling—which may explain this behaviour. In drama two actors may play on stage at the same time two aspects of the same person. The technique has been used to understand how the Nazi doctors in Germany were able to be on one hand model citizens, loving fathers and caring doctors whilst at the same time undertaking some of the most horrendous acts of inhumanity ever inflicted.... (2021, p. 329)

As Severski suggested, the capacity for "doubling" needed to be spontaneous, as professional actors were not suited for this profession.

3. Recruitment processes

> It is well known that a firm's most valuable asset is its people, and this aware-
> ness is even more true for mafias.
> (Catino, 2019, p. 29)

Exchange the word "mafias" for "secret service organizations," and the
statement remains accurate. Indeed, our close look at the practices of
managing secret agents suggests that people are still the most valuable
assets in espionage, despite the ever increasing role of technology. The
Polish agent Vincent Severski made that point in an interview:

> Of course, today, intelligence would not exist without SIGINT,[1] which is used
> to verify important intelligence information. Although Americans have a lot
> of satellites, a lot of state-of-the-art techniques, the CIA has a budget like
> a pretty large country, and even more power—agent intelligence is still the
> most important thing. People are still the most important.[2]

Given the importance of human intelligence, significant effort needs
to be put into recruitment. The first stage in the recruitment process is
defining requirements through the creation of role profiles and personal
specification. In the world of espionage, such requirements change all
the time in line with changes in the geopolitical environment and technological developments. The notion of the enemy changes all the time, and
this determines what skills the potential spies need to possess and what
languages they should speak.

In standard organizations, once a broad pool of possible candidates
has been attracted, the process of selection begins—deciding who should
be recruited. Applications are screened, and various selection methods
considered: interviews, intelligence tests, personality tests, aptitude tests,
or assessment centers. Standard organizations use more and more sophisticated techniques of selection, and artificial intelligence is increasingly

---

[1]   SIGINT is intelligence derived from electronic signals and systems used by
foreign targets, such as communications systems, radars, and weapons systems.
[2]   https://wyborcza.pl/duzyformat/1,127290,17554015,Vincent_V__Sev-
erski__Zona_szpiega_ma_trudniej.html, accessed March 11, 2015, transl. SS.

used to help HR managers make their choices. In the world of espionage, this process might be reversed, as we suggested in the previous chapter. Selection often precedes recruitment, rather than coming at its end: potential candidates might be selected on the basis of covert intelligence gathering and observation and then approached in the hope that they agree to collaborate.

We searched the biographies of spies for descriptions of how they were recruited, and how they recruited others, but also for accounts on how secret service organizations tried to protect themselves against recruitment of their own agents as double agents. However, the circumstances of recruitment of many spies are not known. For example, the biography of the Swedish spy Karin Lannby is unclear about how she was recruited; the author of her biography assumed that she herself took contact, as she offered her services as a translator, but was told that there was no need for such a facility. It is also possible that she took contact again, after the war began (she started her agent's work in October 1939), and mentioned her earlier adventures in France and Spain (Thunberg, 2009).

It should be mentioned that recruitment is one of the areas of managing secret agents where changes over the years have been most evident. A shift away from the informal "tap on the shoulder" to a professionalization agenda has taken place, and the biographies we analyzed in our study have neatly captured this transition.

TAP ON THE SHOULDER

Before the Second World War, and during the war, most secret service organizations could not afford a systematic, professional approach to the recruitment of spies. The biography of Richard Sorge, German spy for the Soviets, reveals that the first generation of Soviet spies had often been failed artists and, in general, "a motley cast of gentlemen amateurs, demi-mondain chancers, opportunists and naive conspirators" (Matthews, 2019, loc. 1013).

In the United Kingdom, MI5 was mainly recruiting well-connected gentlemen from the upper echelons of society who had their own incomes, which meant they didn't rely on payment from the secret service. This suited the secret service as they were said to be surviving on a shoestring: "When the young Dick White [Sir Dick Goldsmith White, Director General of MI5 1953–1956 and of MI6 1956–1968] was sounded out about joining MI5 in 1935, he was told that the pay was poor. 'That's the bad part,' his recruiter said, 'but the good part is, it's tax free'" (Booth, 2007, loc. 604).

In the 1960s, recruitment for MI5 in the United Kingdom was an entirely covert affair, largely dependent on "a haphazard system of talent spotting" (Rimington, 2001, p. 190). Sisman gave an insightful account of David Cornwell's (le Carré) recruitment: it was a tap on the shoulder in the form of invitations for lunch. He was recruited by MI5 while he was working at the British Embassy in Germany.

> David's wanderings took him to the English church in Kirchenfeld (…). There, on Christmas Day, he made the acquaintance of a county lady in tweeds and sensible shoes who introduced herself as "Wendy Gillbanks," and her handsome, chummy, amusing friend "Sandy," both of the Consular Section of the British Embassy. They invited him back for a glass of sherry and a spot of lunch the next day, and gently probed him on his attitudes and beliefs. When the subject of service to one's country came up in the conversation, David was keen to prove himself a patriot, conscious that his father had contributed not very much to the struggle against Hitler. When presented with a legal document pledging him to secrecy—perhaps a version of the Official Secrets Act—at the British Embassy, he had no hesitation in signing. (Sisman, 2015, p. 77)

When Cornwell left MI5 for MI6, he experienced a similar recruitment process. He received "… a letter on Foreign Office notepaper from a vice-admiral, writing from an address in Buckingham Gate, inviting David to lunch with him at the Travellers Club in Pall Mall. (…). Over lunch the Admiral hinted at intelligence work without ever discussing it openly" (Sisman, 2015, p. 136). The tap on the shoulder was, however, supported by information collected, although not always used.

> Later in the year, his tutor W. D. Williams submitted a confidential report in response to a "vetting" enquiry. "David Cornwell has given evidence of ability above the average," he wrote. "He has a discriminating mind with some power and subtlety and a good deal of imagination." In this respect Williams rated him β +. For his character and general suitability to represent his country abroad, Williams rated him higher, α-. "He speaks faultless English and has charm and poise," Williams continued. "He is a thoroughly likeable person, and I should think would get on well with all with whom he came in contact." There is, though, one point which perhaps should be borne in mind. He is of a somewhat unstable disposition, very much inclined to be swept off his feet for a time by some passing enthusiasm, inclined to let generous and idealistic impulses cloud the clarity of his thinking. (…). The authorities at MI6 were aware of David's undercover work for their sister service, and discounted his tutor's warning accordingly. (Sisman, 2015, p. 137)

Here is Stella Rimington's account of her recruitment by MI5:

> One day in the summer of 1967, as I was walking through the High Commission compound, someone tapped me on the shoulder and said, "Psst ... Do you want to be a spy?" What actually happened was that one of the First Secretaries in the High Commission (...) asked me whether, if I had a little spare time on my hands, I might consider helping him out at the office. (...) I went into the High Commission office the next day and he told me that he was the MI5 representative in India and he had more work on hand than he and his secretary could cope with. (...) What was it all about? He gave me a thin paper-backed pamphlet to read, which was probably the only thing in print about MI5 in those days. In about five or six pages, it told me that MI5 was part of the defence forces of the realm, with the special responsibility to protect the country against serious threats to our national security, like espionage and subversion (terrorism had hardly been heard of in those days). (Rimington, 2001, p. 84)

When Rimington decided to rejoin MI5 after her return to London two years later, this time she took the initiative by contacting her baronet friend, who put her in touch with the recruiters. The condition for joining was being positively vetted, which she described to her parents as "little men in bowler hats lurking outside the house" checking on the prospective employee's family and phone calls from "a husky mysterious voice" inquiring whether she "had ever been incarcerated in a prison camp subject to Fascist or Communist influences" (2001, p. 85).

The potential recruit's sexuality mattered in the 1960s, and Cornwell recounted that, under the vetting procedures of the day, gay people were debarred from Secret Service work as they were possibly vulnerable to blackmail. "But the Service seemed quite content to ignore the homosexuals in its own ranks. (...) Yet God help the registry typist whose skirt was deemed too short or too tight, or the married desk officer who gave her the eye" (le Carré, 2016, p. 20).

According to numerous accounts, the covert system of recruitment was not a great success and often produced "unsuitable James Bond lookalikes" (Rimington, 2001, p. 190). In the 1980s, MI5 recognized that the tap-on-the-shoulder method of recruitment posed a real danger of cloning, in that the same types of people were approached and recruited, but they were still not able to seek the advice and resources of the recruitment industry. However, although MI5 still required intelligence officers who were usually generalist graduates, they also needed people with expertise and specific skills: communicators, photographers, linguists, lawyers, and surveillance officers. At this time, such people were still identified and approached covertly, and they were recruited broadly into two types of roles: the "mobiles"—who would peruse the streets, driving or walking, covertly following their targets—and the "statics"—who sat in their observation posts for days and often even nights on end. The mobiles were valued for their alertness and the capacity to merge into the background, but also being able to switch back and forth between periods of inactivity and extreme activity. The statics were required to show a talent for observation and the capacity to maintain their concentration.

> They are very different jobs, but accuracy and the ability to keep awake during the boring bits are vital to both; accurate movement information can make the difference between success and failure in an operation. Identifying selection procedures for the surveillance officers was a challenge and I am sure that we should have taken more external advice than we did. (Rimington, 2001, p. 190)

The method of "tapping on the shoulder" appears to be close to mafias' recruitment method based on kinship (Catino, 2019, p. 294). For secret service organizations, recruited spies may not have been kin in this sense, but they tended to be from the same cultural and class community. With time, and with growing professionalization, both mafias and secret service organizations focused primarily on skills.

Focusing on skills also required a complicated system of testing and vetting. Raymond Palmer (1977), in his account of recruitment procedures in US security agencies, demonstrated how many suitable candidates from the best universities were eventually found unsuitable. "Talent spotters," usually friendly professors, were used to identify the best achieving students, who were then screened by the CIA. Palmer quoted an illustrative example: a thousand potential recruits from the top quarter of their classes at US universities (mainly Ivy League—Princeton, Harvard, and Yale) were targeted, and 800 screened out immediately because of their unfavorable background and lack of educational standards. Some 200 usually went through security checks and personality assessments and then the number reduced to 90 because 70 showed "personal defects such as drinking, talking too much or homosexuality (sic!)" (Palmer 1977, p. 30), and 40 were dropped for security reasons. Of the 90 who remained, 10 would not take up the offer and the other 80 would be enrolled in the training program. The success rate after that was also poor: 2–3 would decide it wasn't for them, 4–5 would be judged as not cut out for the job, and 8–9 would be regarded as doubtful. "Out of a possible 1000 recruits, then, probably around 70 would make the grade" (Palmer, 1977, p. 31).

VOLUNTEERING FOR THE JOB

If selection preceded recruitment, and recruitment depended on either "kinship" or "skills," it seems unlikely that anybody would be able to volunteer to be a spy. Yet, Eddie Chapman "volunteered" for the German secret service while he was a British agent, thus becoming a British double agent.

> Chapman and Faramus composed a letter in carefully wrought German, and sent it to the German Command post in St Helier, addressed to General Otto von Stulpnägel, the senior officer in command of the occupation forces in France and the Channel Islands. A few days later Faramus and Chapman were summoned to the office of a German major, where Chapman blithely explained that he and his friend would like to join the German secret service. He listed his crimes, stressed the outstanding warrants he faced in Britain, emphasised his expertise with explosives, and concluded with a spirited anti-British rant. (Macintyre, 2007, pp. 28–29)

Most biographies we read, including that of Chapman, suggest that there was a degree of skepticism about people who offered themselves to the secret service. In Chapman's case, it seemed that a long-standing principle was activated—that anyone who applies to join a secret service should be rejected. After he offered his help to the Germans, he did not hear from them for a while. Eventually, though, Chapman was asked about his motivation, which was, allegedly, both his hatred of Britain and the promise of financial gain. When offered the job, Chapman agreed on the spot (Macintyre, 2007, p. 38). As it turned out, the Abwehr had been searching for someone like that for months—an Englishman without scruples, "adept at concealment, intelligent, ruthless and mercenary" (2007, p. 45)—and preferably someone with a criminal background.

Financial remuneration had to be used sparingly, as a sudden injection of cash could give the spy away. Such concerns arose when Ashraf Marwan was recruited by Mossad. His biographer noted, "It was clear that an infusion of cash could translate into a suddenly profligate lifestyle—raising questions about whether he was selling state secrets. The Mossad had faced this problem in the past, but the amounts were always small and the agents extremely careful" (Bar-Joseph, 2017, p. 51).

Kim Philby did not exactly volunteer his services to MI6, but when he decided that he wanted to work for them (he was a good journalist, but wanted something more from life), he dropped a few hints to his friends, and very soon someone approached him with an offer (Macintyre, 2014).

TOWARD THE PROFESSIONALIZATION AGENDA

Some biographers offered detailed accounts of recruitment, even those undertaken during the Second World War. For example, the recruitment of Krystyna Skarbek, a Polish spy working for Britain, was described as follows:

> Krystyna was interviewed by a Major Gielgud.[3] She later discovered that he was the brother of Sir John Gielgud. The major was delighted by the clarity and detail of the reporting from this astonishingly attractive young woman. Krystyna said the Germans behaved like bullies when they moved in packs, but pissed in their pants when separated from their pals, and shat in their pants if attacked singly. She proposed, with great passion, ways to reinforce Polish morale, and to let them know they were not forgotten. Gielgud passed her over to Vera. The two spoke the same language: sabotage, subversion, scare the shit out of the Germans. Krystyna said she was able to return to Poland by skiing over the mountains. She could send back reports through Budapest, where she had friends who were able to travel freely in Hungary, and even Austria. Vera arranged for Krystyna to be based in Budapest, and to be paid the equivalent in today's money of $10,000 over a six-month period as a news correspondent. (Stevenson, 2011, p. 161)

Eli Cohen's recruitment was unconventional: Mossad's Director General, Meir Amit, who was looking for an agent to infiltrate the Syrian government, found his name in the agency's files of rejected candidates, as none of the current candidates were suitable. Cohen was put under surveillance and after two weeks informed that Mossad had decided to recruit him. He then took a six-month course at the Mossad training school.

Marwan was recruited in the period leading up to the 1973 Arab–Israel War, after suspicions that he was an Egyptian spy had been removed.

> After examining the problem from every angle, the group concluded that the chances were low that Marwan was other than what he seemed. There were three main reasons. First, because only the most sophisticated spy agencies knew how to operate double agents successfully over time. The British were

---

[3]   The Gielguds were of Polish–Lithuanian descent on their father's side.

the best at it, especially during World War II. The Soviets were pretty good as well, though not as good as the British. The Mossad understood the difficulties involved and refrained from deploying double agents entirely. The only Israeli agency that used them was the Shin Bet, and their experience was limited. The Egyptian Mukhabarat was not known for being especially sophisticated. Their efforts to infiltrate Israel with spies had made them out to be a fairly amateur organization whose best successes were in crushing opposition within Egypt itself. The Mossad officers were hesitant to underestimate their enemies, but they had difficulty giving the Egyptians credit that, according to their own professional opinions, they didn't deserve. (Bar-Joseph, 2017, p. 49)

It wasn't until 1996 that new openness initiatives were introduced in the United Kingdom, and MI5 professionalized their recruitment. The organization designed a new recruitment strategy and used the services of the Civil Service Selection Board to help in the selection of graduates, searching for a mix of qualities and talents. Since 1997, advertisements for staff have appeared in newspapers and journals. Rimington recalled the following:

We wanted people with a good brain, good analytical skills, the ability to sort out information and put it in order and to express themselves well orally and on paper. But coupled with that they needed to be self-starting, with a warm personality and the ability to persuade. And we needed people who would be good on their feet in difficult and possibly dangerous operational situations, where they could not seek advice. We also wanted common sense, balance and integrity. It's quite a tall order. (2001, p. 190)

MI5 were constantly refining their selection tests to try to identify graduates with the right qualities, but over time they understood that some of those qualities were rather difficult to detect in young people, whose talents—not to mention personalities —were not fully developed.

We didn't always get the recruiting right, who does? For a time we recruited too many people with intellectual skills, but not enough practical skills, and that resulted in a crisis when we were overweighted with excellent assessment abilities but had too few people capable of gathering the raw material, the intelligence, to assess. Occasionally we recruited people who simply lacked the necessary judgement and common sense. The problem for secret organisations is that getting recruitment wrong can have more far-reaching effects than in other fields. (ibid.)

A move toward professionalization was also evident in the more contemporary recruitment accounts of Polish espionage. When Filip Hagenbeck, the former leader of the Polish secret service's Counterintelligence

Branch 10, finished his military service in 1978, he applied to the Ministry of Internal Affairs (Hagenbeck, 2019). Recommendation was provided by his father's colleague, high up in the party. He was invited to an interview with a staff member. A man met him at the entrance and led him to the Independent Personnel Section. Questions were asked. Does he know English? Yes. Who recommended him? Hagenbeck didn't know, just that it was some acquaintance of his father. The interviewer said he would find out. Was Hagenbeck ready for a nine-month training outside Warsaw? Yes, but what about a wife and two daughters? No contacts at the beginning; then only during holidays and birthdays.

After a family meeting, during which his mother promised to take care of his younger daughter, Hagenbeck returned to the recruiter and was told to take medical and then psychological tests. He couldn't find the clinic and was a few minutes late. He was greeted by a psychologist: "Someone just died because of you! You came late to an important meeting!" Then he took various tests, including intelligence tests.

Severski, too, mentioned the need for psychiatric examinations at the recruitment stage, when it seems lying is easily spotted, as seen in the following:

I: And if a candidate comes and lies?
S: We know immediately. If in tests he exaggerates his competences, he falls out. Or, some young people come and say: "I want to work in intelligence, this is my dream because I hate these Islamists or these Russians." When we hear something like this, we don't even meet them for the second time. The spy can't hate anyone. The spy loves his homeland, nothing more.[4]

Jennifer duBois was recruited by the CIA via advertisement but decided to choose a writing career instead. Reflecting on the recruitment process, she noticed strong similarities between the two occupations: "an interest in psychology, a facility with narrative, a tendency to position oneself as an observer, and a willingness to lie and call it something else."[5] She applied online, and a few weeks later the CIA contacted her by telephone. After a short interview—that went poorly in her opinion—she received a request for written material, and she sent essays. She was called to an interview and information session in Boston, where she was asked

---

[4] https://wyborcza.pl/duzyformat/1,127290,17554015,Vincent_V__Severski__Zona_szpiega_ma_trudniej.html, accessed March 11, 2015, transl. SS.
[5] duBois (2016).

to rank the significance of various objects in a hypothetical scenario. She received a recommended book list from the CIA, all of them on the agency's operation, and not all of them flattering. Later, she was invited to Washington for a further three-day interview.

She was also advised to consider carefully who, if anybody, should be informed of her application (she said her mother and her boyfriend); friends and acquaintances were told that she was applying for a job with the State Department. During the interviews (there were several rounds) she was encouraged to ask questions, one of which regarded how to avoid talking about sensitive matters and how to change the subject. She was required to deliver memorized briefings (on political issues of her choice), as well as undergo a battery of tests and follow-up conversations with the CIA psychiatrist. After she received a conditional offer of employment, the CIA started a security investigation. The investigator, a middle-aged woman, "interviewed my childhood friends and their parents, my boyfriend and his startled roommates. She asked them about my international trips and foreign national contacts and whether I'd been known to smoke marijuana (…) She drove to my hometown, several hours west, to interview my mother. While I was there over winter break, a car tailed me for twenty minutes, late at night, through the deserted woods" (duBois, 2016). In the end, duBois decided to start a writers' workshop instead and "self-cancelled" her CIA application via fax.

RECRUITMENT OF DOUBLE AGENTS

Becoming a double agent has a particular cachet; still, Spanish spy Juan Pujol García's (Garbo) case was unique because he self-recruited for both Germany and Britain.

Before offering his services to the Nazis, he thoroughly studied their doctrines. Then he phoned the German embassy in Madrid and asked if he could talk to the military attaché. "They suggested I ring back the next day, when they would give me an answer" (García and West, 2011, pp. 49–50). García finally convinced his contact at the embassy that the Abwehr should recruit him.

> I was personally convinced at the time that he [Federico, a German contact] had recruited me on the advice of his superiors; I am equally convinced that, intoxicated by my verbosity, he personally fought for all my suggestions, projects and plans and warmly recommended them to his superiors. But why he had such blind faith in me I do not know. Whatever the truth of the matter, a few weeks after our first meeting, he brought me a bottle of invisible ink,

some secret codes and the sum of $3,000, making sure that I had them in good time before I left for Britain. Then he briefed me about the kind of reports they expected me to send them. (García and West, 2011, p. 58)

He observed, as follows, that it was much harder to convince the British to take him on as a double agent:

All my attempts to hand over my valuable new acquisitions, my ink and my codes, failed; I was quite unable to reach anyone of importance whom I felt I could trust at the British embassy. After all that I had done, all that I had gone through, all the subterfuges I'd invented, the deceptions and the chicanery, the tension and the strain, let alone all the time I had spent, I was no further forward than I had been when I made my first attempt. It seemed utterly incredible and was the most bitter disappointment to me. I just could not understand why the British were so difficult when the Germans were so understanding and cooperative. Why, I kept on asking myself, was the enemy proving to be so helpful, while those whom I wanted to be my friends were being so implacable? (García and West, 2011, p. 89)

Finally, it was agreed that he should be invited to travel to London and continue under MI5's supervision. The potential prize of a direct line into the enemy's intelligence was too tempting.

Jonason and Olsson described the way in which Wulf Schmidt (Tate)—later also known as Harry Williamson, a double agent working for Britain against Germany—was recruited by the Germans:

In 1938, Danish-born Wulf Schmidt returned to Germany because he had been informed that his former employer was offering work in Argentina. But the borders of the South American countries were closed. (...) In 1940, Wulf came to Hamburg where he received orders to go to the local immigration office to register. (Jonason and Olsson, 2011, p. 7)

An officer who met Schmidt told him that he had a friend, Doctor Scholtz, who most likely would be interested in Schmidt's experiences in Africa, even to the point of offering him a job, and promised to arrange a meeting.

At the meeting, Dr Scholtz (...) wanted to hear about Wulf's background, but seemed, to Wulf's disappointment, quite uninterested in his travels and experiences in Argentina and Cameroon. Apparently more interesting was what he had observed in various ports. (...) A few days later, Scholtz said that a company in Copenhagen could employ [Schmidt], and he was going to be sent to England on the firm's behalf. When he came back he should report everything he saw and heard about the morale of the people, and the food situation. The trip was, however, cancelled, and soon afterwards, on 9 April 1940, Denmark was invaded by the Germans. After that, he was instructed to travel to Denmark on a mission of espionage. (Jonason and Olsson, 2011, p. 8)

Jonason and Olsson also described how double agents were sourced by the British among German detainees:

> During the interrogations [at Camp 020 in the United Kingdom], the goal was to clarify whether the detainees (captured German agents) were guilty, to get as much vital information about enemy intentions as possible, and to recruit inmates as double agents in the Double-Cross system. The development of interrogation methodology at Latchmere relied a lot on "trial and error," and accumulated experience; there were no pre-written manuals on the subject. (2011, p. 18)

There was a clear rule that physical violence was not to be used during the interrogations—in any circumstance. The quality of information received this way was doubtful; also, the recruiters did not want to use brutal "Gestapo methods." A sophisticated psychological intimidation, on the other hand, was frequently deployed:

> ... the classic technique of "good cop, bad cop" was used, particularly if the inmate (enemy agent) was considered more susceptible to a gentleman's approach. The first interview was with a terse threat of a death sentence (...), and the prisoner was sent away without the opportunity of defending himself. Later, a more sympathetic officer arrived in the cell, and tried to smooth over the harsh statements of the first hearing if the prisoner was willing to cooperate. After the agent had admitted his espionage mission it often seemed as if a burden had eased, and many were willing to cooperate fully. Several agreed to switch to an active role in the Allied service, or as "stool pigeons" or "sympathy men" in the camp. (2011, p. 21)

The recruitment of double agents required paying attention to the distinction between those who were "turned" and those who volunteered their services.

> In recent accounts of the double-cross system insufficient distinction has been made between those agents who volunteered their services, and were therefore trusted entirely, and those who had operated after a measure of duress, and were therefore kept in secure accommodation under constant surveillance. Considerable attention has been given to the latter variety (...) because of the challenge they had initially presented to their interrogators. Of the four most successful MI5 double agents, Brutus, Mutt, Tate and Garbo, only Tate

possessed the motivation to resist. All the others were already ideologically suited to the turning process and had never intended to genuinely complete their mission for the Abwehr. Garbo's case was to be unique because he had specifically set out to become a double agent. None of the others nurtured such a dangerous ambition and only stumbled into the espionage arena unintentionally. (García and West, 2011, pp. 63–64)

Philby was approached by a Soviet agent, Arnold Deutsch, and invited to work as a double agent for the Soviet Union, but he wasn't exactly "turned"; he had developed communist sympathies while studying at Cambridge University and was excited to work for the inner ring— whatever the organization.

At their second meeting, Deutsch asked Philby if he was willing to act as an undercover agent for the communist cause. Philby did not hesitate: "One does not look twice at an offer of enrolment in an elite force," he wrote. That was a most telling remark: the attraction of this new role lay in its exclusivity. In some ways, Philby's story is that of a man in pursuit of ever more exclusive clubs. (Macintyre, 2014, p. 40)

This pursuit has been described by many commentators as specifically British, but it could also be applied to agents of other nationalities. Belonging to an elite group is seen as attractive by many, and perhaps especially by those with a craving to be appreciated.

RECRUITING THE INFORMANTS

Once recruited and established in their jobs, agents were often in charge of recruiting others into their network. This activity, too, had its complications. For example, the Germans trusted García to recruit his informants, but they were largely fictional.

Pujol developed his own network of [invented] sub-agents. Pujol's most experienced agent, and future deputy, was designated Agent THREE, a wealthy Venezuelan student named Carlos. In order to protect his identity, the Abwehr always referred to him in their secret communications by the code name Benedict. These, of course, were routinely intercepted at Hanslope Park and decrypted. Benedict allegedly lived in Glasgow and had promised to recruit his own subagents in the north of England. (García and West, 2011, p. 101)

The MI5 officer who controlled Eddie Chapman (Zigzag) was against letting him recruit his own informants as "they did not want to encourage Eddie's contacts with the criminal fraternity. And in the event, Eddie was able to claim that 'the friends he hoped to employ for this purpose are in prison or otherwise not available'" (Booth, 2007, loc. 5172–5179).

Certain elements of the recruitment procedures are similar to those used in standard organizations—candidates are tested and interviewed, their credentials checked, and their personality suitability verified. There are many differences, though, and these are most evident in the recruitment of double agents. Most striking is the atmosphere of distrust surrounding recruitment. Entering into the role of a double agent may carry the risk of becoming a triple agent. Layers upon layers of deception and suspicion require stringent verification and double-checking. After all, recruiting the wrong person may have serious consequences.

4. The Office

There were many offices of secret service organizations in numerous different countries but there were also subdivisions within the same country. Take the United Kingdom, for example, where MI5, MI6, and SOE are perhaps best known to the general public; they also serve as good illustrations of a common problem for intelligence units: cooperation.

UNITED KINGDOM

The origins of MI5 and MI6 and their bosses' pseudonyms are well described by Stella Rimington in her autobiography (2001). By 1909, the UK government realized that to successfully counter German espionage, they had to find out what foreign agents were doing in Britain and then try to stop them in their tracks. They also needed to send their own secret agents to Germany, so that any dangerous plans could be thwarted before it was too late. A Working Group was established with a remit to set up a Secret Service Bureau, and two officers were "plucked out of the armed services and told to get on with it" (Rimington, 2001, p. 72).

> One was Captain Vernon Kell of the South Staffordshire Regiment, who was at the time working on an intelligence desk in the Committee of Imperial Defence, and had made his reputation as a Chinese expert. The other, Captain Mansfield Cumming of the Royal Navy, was formerly Boom Defence Officer at Southampton. (...) Kell took the home end, responsibility for counter-espionage work within the British Isles, finding out what the spies were doing here in Britain, while Cumming (...) took responsibility for gathering information overseas—and MI5 and MI6 were born. (2001, p. 83)

Rimington also explained that, as a result, the head of counterespionage in MI5 had until recently been called "K," after Kell, while the chief of MI6 was still known as "C," after Cumming. "M" was someone else, in contrast to what James Bond fans believed.

MI5 (the Agency Specializing in Counterespionage)

MI5 was a secret service, operating murkily in the shadows, often beyond the law. Lies, subterfuge and deception were its stock in trade. It was possible for British intelligence to round up a network of spies without a word leaking out. [Whereas] when the FBI rounded up a spy network in the United States, it made front-page headlines. (Miller, 2004, loc. 2765)

Such secrecy appeared excessive in the view of David Cornwell (le Carré], who worked for both MI5 and MI6 during the 1950s and 1960s. When he first joined MI5, "[t]o a young recruit like David, much of what went on in the Office seemed ludicrous anyway. (…) New recruits curious about the identity of their mysterious employers were fobbed off—'just the War Office, old boy'" (Sisman, 2015, p. 192).

Rimington, who served as Director General of MI5 from 1992 to 1996, quickly learned that "people regarded you with suspicion if you asked too many questions" (2001, p. 98). Indeed, when she first joined MI5, she was not even certain whether she was supposed to know the name of the Director General. "There was a joke going around that you would know which was the Director-General because he was the one who always wore his dark glasses indoors so that he would not be recognised" (ibid.).

In her autobiography, Rimington gave a balanced assessment of the need for secrecy. To begin with, she emphasized its importance given the life-and-death nature of the operations:

Information was, very properly, held tightly and there was a series of circles within circles. As a newcomer, you were in the very outer circle, but as you carried out your day-to-day tasks you became aware that there were lots of other circles of which you were not a member. (…) This system was necessary, as some of the human sources whose identity it was protecting were at risk of imprisonment or death should their activities be revealed. And there was the ever-present fear that one of us might be a spy, a penetration agent for the Soviet bloc. (2001, p. 114)

However, she also commented on the excessive secrecy, and its damage to organizational trust and loyalty:

Every organisation has to cope with the problems of confidentiality but in MI5 this issue exists in an extreme form. Everyone, even the most lowly member of staff, has some secret information in their head, or available to them, which could cause damage if leaked. So rigorous and intrusive security checks are required, not only when staff join in the first place, but regularly throughout their career. But at the same time it is important to avoid any sense of mutual suspicion. On the contrary, what must be generated is mutual trust and loyalty, because the success of any operation depends on teams working closely together, and people's lives may be in the hands of their colleagues. (2001, p. 188)

In Cornwell's days the Director General was Roger Hollis, a shy, kindly man who allegedly resembled an undertaker, always dressed in a black jacket and striped trousers. Despite being one of the most junior officers, Cornwell spent a fair amount of time with Hollis, carrying his bag at meetings with Chief Constables in regional cities or sitting at the back of the room when operations were being proposed.

Hollis had to cope with the repercussions from a series of spy scandals. Such scandals, and various doubtful revelations of Soviet defectors, would convince some of the MI5 officers that the organization had been penetrated at a high level. Their suspicions had been confirmed by the CIA's Chief of Counterintelligence, James Jesus Angleton, who had a habit of suspecting everybody, including Henry Kissinger (Rimington, 2001). One possible explanation for this tendency was the humiliation inflicted upon Angleton by Kim Philby's numerous acts of betrayal; it was Philby who trained Angleton in the art of running double agents.[1] This atmosphere of suspicion paralyzed MI5, producing a climate in which nothing and nobody could be trusted. Following his retirement in 1965, Hollis was summoned back to MI5 and interrogated by his former subordinates. In the 1980s, testimony from a senior KGB defector, Oleg Gordievsky, revealed that the Soviets themselves were baffled by the allegations against Hollis and attributed these to "some mysterious, internal British intrigue" (Sisman, 2015, p. 192).

During its more successful period of operation, that is, during the Second World War, MI5 had several groups and committees with specific tasks and responsibilities (some of which included members from other organizations). Here we present some of the best known.

The XX Committee
Ready to act by the end of 1940, the XX Committee, or Twenty Committee, "was to run what became known as 'the great game of double cross' for the remainder of the war" (Miller, 2004, loc. 133). It was created due to a demand for more coherence and control in the

---

[1]   Michael Holzman (2021) claims, however, that Angleton was justified in being obsessive and that his zeal did more good than bad.

complex management of double agents during the Second World War. The increasing number of double agents (pretending to work for the Abwehr) recruited by MI5 meant a greater need for control and management. "There was a need for an all-embracing body, which controlled and directed the activities, and had a comprehensive overview of the various double agents' fictitious businesses, with a coherent structure of information flow without contradictions" (Jonason and Olsson, 2011, p. 36).

The XX Committee apparently fulfilled this need very well. The activities of each agent were monitored by the Committee, but the responsibility for the day-to-day running of spies was given to an individual MI5 officer. Another task of the Committee was to obtain the cooperation of the relevant services to supply suitable material for the agent to give to the enemy (García and West, 2011).

In January 1941, the Committee's Chairman, John C. Masterman, called the members to the first meeting. Under his leadership, the Committee prepared a plan that would permit different parts of British Intelligence to work together for their common task—"to fool the Germans by playing on their worst fears" (Booth, 2007, loc. 1109–1116).

The members of the Committee represented several different organizations: MI5, MI6, the War Office, Air Ministry Intelligence, the Naval Intelligence Department, the London Controlling Section (LCS, with a mandate to coordinate deception plans during the Second World War), the Chief of Combined Operations, and the Supreme Headquarters Allied Expeditionary Force (SHAEF), the global body for Allied forces' military cooperation. "A total of 226 meetings were held before the war ended. The committee managed almost always to reach a decision through consensus. (…) During the war about 120 double agents were handled, with varying degrees of activity, most with only a minor role" (Jonason and Olsson, 2011, pp. 36–37).

From the beginning of 1944, all the resources of the XX Committee were devoted to Operation Fortitude, a military deception deployed by the Allies in the build-up to the Normandy Landings of the same year. Fortitude was designed to mislead the Germans regarding the location of the invasion. This was an incredibly complex operation, with high stakes. Case officers had daily meetings at SHAEF to produce the false information that would be fed to the enemy. "The risks were horrendous. If one piece failed to fit, the whole charade could be exposed, leading to the danger that the Germans would start reading the agents' message 'in reverse' and thereby accurately divine Allied intentions" (Miller, 2004, loc. 4192–4199).

For campaigns, subcommittees were created, for example, the so-called 212 Committee, whose task was to facilitate communications between the commanders in the field in France and MI5's case officers (García and West, 2011, p. 170). But the XX Committee rarely dealt directly with German agents—this was the responsibility of Section B1A.

Section B1A

Its task was "catching enemy spies, turning them, and then running them as double agents" (Macintyre, 2007, pp. 67–68), and it was run by Tommy "Tar" Robertson. Arrested agents were taken to Camp 020 at Latchmere House, in Richmond, South West London, previously used as a convalescent home for officers during the First World War (Miller, 2004). Camp 020 was run by Lieutenant Colonel Robin "Tin Eye" Stephens.

The members of Section B1A were sometimes called "a team of gifted amateurs," as they included "lawyers, academics, an industrialist, a circus owner, at least one artist, an art dealer and a poet" (Macintyre, 2007, p. 70). Nevertheless, they played a significant role in the double-cross operations: "B1A's ever-expanding stable of real and notional agents had completely eliminated every independent German spy and had enabled the port security staff to prepare reception committees for new arrivals" (García and West, 2011, pp. 70–71).

However, Guy Liddell, Deputy Director General of MI5, remained uncertain about Section B1A's efficacy. In his opinion, it "had degenerated into a duplication of the Twenty Committee. At best, it dealt with a few ad hoc questions put up to it but it never gave any direction on matters of major policy, one of the purposes for which it was originally set up" (West, 2005a, p. 233). Evidently, a new organization was needed.

London Controlling Section (LCS)

In 1942, control of the double-cross operation was handed to this highly secret unit. The LCS got off to a faltering start, as bureaucracy increased, and their task—trying to deceive the Germans about an invasion of Norway instead of North Africa—was generally seen as rather far-fetched (Jonason and Olsson, 2011). In the same vein, agent Juan Pujol García's (Garbo) network was asked to persuade the Germans that the south coast of England was teeming with men from a nonexistent Sixth Army (García and West, 2011).

SHAEF, however, fared much better.

SHAEF

This was the global body for Allied military cooperation, under the command of US General Dwight Eisenhower. Ops B, in turn, was a deception planning department within SHAEF, operating under the direction of Colonel Noel Wild after he replaced Colonel Jervis-Read in 1943. Ops B was divided into two sections: one dealt with physical deception, such as camouflage; the other handled various forms of controlled leakage.

The Wireless Board

This was a special committee drawn from all Allied armed services and was meant to coordinate the activities of double agents. Thanks to the Board's operations, by December 1940 MI5 could analyze the wireless traffic of their agents. The Board was able to construct a message and then watch and intercept its receipt and acknowledgment in Hamburg, followed by its recoding and further transmission to Berlin (García and West, 2011). The Board even created an offshoot, "a subgroup of specialist intelligence officers to develop the double-cross system further and coordinate the real and notional activities of their charges" (García and West, 2011, p. 66).

Radio Security Service (RSS)

The RSS was established by MI5 in 1939 to detect and monitor enemy radio transmissions. Arthur Watts, President of the Radio Society of Great Britain, recruited radio amateurs with advanced Morse skills, who became known as the Voluntary Interceptors. The RSS was regarded as a vital tool, becoming a part of MI8 (Military Intelligence) in December 1941.

If the organization of the MI5 office seems rather complicated, this impression was certainly shared by its Deputy Director, Guy Liddell, who, in 1939, had long discussions

> ... with Jack Curry and Richman Stopford about office organisation. I have a strong feeling that although we have a few good cases going, we are mainly sifting information which reaches us with the kind assistance of the general public. There is very little attempt to use imagination or make a real drive to collect *agents provocateurs*. We are of course up against many difficulties, not the least of which is trying to follow people in the black-out, but the present means for investigation which are at our disposal seem to be very meagre and when we come to the provinces, we are often completely up against it. (West, 2005a, p. 50)

These discussions ended with the formation of the O Branch, specifically to deal with organization.

Rimington reported feeling struck by how "old-fashioned and eccentric" MI5 was when she arrived there in 1969 and stated that its "ethos had not changed very much from the days when a small group of military officers, all male of course and all close colleagues working in great secrecy, pitted their wits against the enemy" (2001, p. 105). Part of that old-fashioned ethos was a strict sex discrimination policy and segregation of women's and men's jobs.

> It did not matter that I had a degree, that I had worked for several years already in the public service, at a higher grade than they were offering, or that I was thirty-four years old. The policy was that men were recruited as what were called "officers" and women had their own career structure, a second-class career, as "assistant officers." They did all sorts of support work—collating, indexing, ensuring the papers were filed in the right place and simple, straightforward enquiries, but not the sharp-end intelligence-gathering operations. (ibid.)

Women could not work as agent-runners or as recruiters of human sources of information, the rationale being that no officer would take instruction from a woman.

> The theory was, and of course it had never been tested, that no KGB officer or foreign intelligence officer of any kind would take direction from a woman. Moreover, the theory went, you certainly could not put a woman to make direct contact with someone from an Arab country, because the cultural differences were too extreme for that to work. Nor was the Irish terrorist target suitable work for a woman. Again the cultural differences were too great, and in any case it was dangerous, and dangerous work was not for women. It was even said that women could not work in sections where they would have to deal a lot with the police, as policemen would not take women seriously as colleagues. (2001, p. 134)

Rimington also recalled the often dull nature of trainees' intelligence work, which consisted of accurate recording of files and monitoring rural branches of the Communist Party. Only later in their careers did MI5 officers experience the more exciting aspects of espionage, resonant of John le Carré novels.

> Foreign intelligence officers were leaving packets of money in hollow trees on Hampstead Heath or, more frequently, in the Home Counties, for their agents, in exchange for secret documents left behind loose bricks in walls; they were

communicating with them by making chalk marks on lamp posts or by leaving empty drinks cans on the top of walls, just as he describes. (Rimington, 2001, p. 153)

Apparently, the habits acquired during the service years remained for the rest of agents' lives:

> If ever I see a jogger in the park apparently spraining his ankle or a dog suddenly keel over and look sick, I look carefully at the scene to see if I can make out a likely target there and detect at work the successors of those agent-running officers of the 1970s. (Rimington, 2001, p. 143)

Such facets of the job may appear exciting when fictionalized, but Rimington emphasized that getting it wrong could cost lives, and the pressure caused agents a deal of stress. Cognizant of such strain, MI5 bosses eventually created the post of Staff Counsellor—an outsider to the intelligence services, to whom employees could talk in confidence if they had anxieties about their work or any other problem that they did not want to discuss with their line managers. One such difficulty was maintaining a somewhat normal life outside work, for example, making and keeping friends or maintaining relationships with neighbors, in a situation where one had to be secretive about one's job.

MI6 (Secret Intelligence Service, SIS)

SIS was founded in 1909 as a section of the Secret Service Bureau and became known for intelligence gathered by means of interpersonal contacts during the Second World War. As le Carré's biographer, Adam Sisman, observed, there is a clear distinction between MI5 and MI6:

> The function of MI5, as set out in a 1952 Directive from the Home Secretary that became regarded as its charter, is "the Defence of the Realm as a whole, from external and internal dangers arising from attempts of espionage and sabotage, or from the actions of persons and organizations, whether directed from within or without the country, which may be judged to be subversive of the state." MI5 operates on home territory, which in those days included the colonies of the British Empire. The function of MI6, on the other hand, is to collect secret intelligence and mount covert operations overseas. Another way of looking at the difference between the two organisations is that MI5 is essentially defensive, whereas MI6 is offensive. MI5 is answerable to the Home Secretary, MI6 to the Foreign Secretary. (Sisman, 2015, pp. 194–195)

In practice, however, some overlap was essential between the two intelligence services, but there was also rivalry and mistrust, at times bordering on hostility. Before Cornwell (le Carré) joined MI6, and while he was working for MI5, like his colleagues he referred to MI6 as "Those Sods Across the Park—a reference to its headquarters on the far side of St James's Park" (Sisman, 2015, p. 195). But earlier on, during the Second World War, bad feeling was not limited to external sources. "Like many small, sealed, self-replicating communities, MI6 was riven with internecine feuding. Its senior officers loathed each other, and intrigued ferociously" (Macintyre, 2014, p. 50).

However, according to Nicholas Elliott, MI6 officer and friend of Philby, the general atmosphere was positive. He was sworn to secrecy outside, whereas inside "the secular monastery" of MI6, he was among people he could trust and speak to openly.

> "It was an organisation in which a large proportion of one's colleagues, male and female, were personal friends," wrote Elliott. "A sort of convivial camaraderie prevailed, rather like a club, in which we all called each other by our first names, and saw a lot of one another outside the office." (Macintyre, 2014, p. 25)

Philby, a double agent for the Soviet Union, began working for MI6 in 1940. He joined Section D, which had been established in 1938 to investigate possible ways of attacking enemies by nonmilitary means. When he started, Philby reported to a building near the MI6 headquarters; he was installed in an office and given paper, pencil, and a telephone. Allegedly he did nothing for two weeks, except read the newspapers and have long, liquid lunches with Guy Burgess, another member of the Cambridge Five spy ring that operated from the mid-1930s to the early years of the Cold War era.

Philby's time at Section D was short-lived. He was soon assigned to Brickendonbury Hall, a secret school for spies in Hertfordshire, where émigré Czechs, Belgians, Norwegians, Dutchmen, and Spaniards were being trained for covert operations. This unit would later be absorbed into the SOE (Macintyre, 2014, p. 20).

SOE

The SOE (Special Operations Executive) was formed in 1940 to conduct espionage, sabotage, and reconnaissance in occupied Europe. It soon became known as "Churchill's Secret Army." The SOE's tasks were closely related to those of MI6 (SIS), which was a cause of some tension: "Malcolm Muggeridge, the writer and a wartime spy, observed that although SOE and the SIS were on the same side, they were more abhorrent to one another than they were to the German intelligence corps, the Abwehr" (Stevenson, 2011, p. 141).

A key figure in the SOE was the so-called spymistress Vera Atkins. In the years leading up to the Second World War, Atkins provided Winston Churchill with information on Germany's secret preparations for a blitzkrieg; this was at a time when Churchill was in the political wilderness, seen by some as a drunkard and warmonger. Later, in the mid-1940s, he was suddenly in charge of a war that seemed already lost. This was when he officially founded the SOE, an intelligence agency that was to specialize in nontraditional methods. Atkins's principal role was the recruitment and deployment of British agents in occupied France, with specific responsibility for female SOE agents, and "SOE's structure was so fluid that even if she chose to wear the modest uniform of a pilot-officer, she could still give orders to a major general" (Stevenson, 2011, p. 142).

The SOE was to represent "tangle within tangle, plot and counter-plot, ruse and treachery, cross and double-cross, true agent, false agent, double agent" (Stevenson, 2011, p. 321). It was also the source of various clandestine bodies, such as the Political Warfare Executive (PWE) formed in August 1941 to produce and disseminate propaganda, with the aim of damaging enemy morale and sustaining the morale of countries occupied by Nazi Germany. The PWE's "most controversial boss was Sir Bruce Lockhart, convicted as a British spy in Russia and exchanged for a prominent Soviet prisoner in 1918. He was known as a man of action, irritated by some aspects of secret agencies, where—he wrote later—'most of the energy which should be directed against the enemy is dissipated in interdepartmental strife and jealousies'" (Stevenson, 2011, p. 165).

Interdepartmental Strife

Such interdepartmental strife became a concern for Liddell, who was anxious about the effects on the SIS of a potential US version of the SOE: "It is bad enough having an English SOE but if there is to be an American one as well I fear there may be a major disaster" (West, 2005a, p. 196). Liddell met with two representatives of the CIA, one of whom told him

> ... that he now had a mandate from the Chiefs of Staff to start up an organi-
> sation covering the activities of SIS, SOE, PWE and ourselves in Europe, the
> Middle East and Far East. He wanted to know whether in his outstations he
> should make one person head of all four organisations or whether they should
> communicate separately to headquarters in Washington DC. I said that from
> our experience I was quite certain that he ought to place the four departments
> under one head, otherwise they would undoubtedly get across each other's
> tracks and the work of one might well be damaging to the others. (West,
> 2005a, p. 263)

Liddell was a confirmed advocate for a full exchange of information between different organizations dealing with German intelligence. He added that he

> ... felt that in the best of worlds we should both be houses in the same office
> but that since for a variety of reasons this had not been considered possible, we
> had to strive for the next best thing, namely complete and frank interchange of
> information on all questions affecting the German intelligence service. (West,
> 2005a, p. 194)

This feeling was widely shared among the top MI5 officers, who saw a need for close cooperation, especially between MI5 and MI6. Yet, the relationship between the two organizations has been fraught with tensions practically from the outset. According to Miller, "Problems initially stemmed from a marked reluctance by each organisation to share information with the other, but natural rivalry and jealousy also contributed to the tension" (2004, loc. 270). They disagreed on most issues (e.g., on whether Philby was a traitor), due to "their famed rivalry," as Hanning (2021, p. 36) put it. Such a situation was not limited to the United Kingdom.

GERMANY

The Abwehr

The Abwehr (German for "defense") was the German military intelligence service for the Reichswehr and Wehrmacht from 1920 to 1945.

Wilhelm Canaris, Chief of the Abwehr from 1935 to 1944, reported directly to the German High Command.

> The work of Section B1A and the XX Committee was made immeasurably easier by the fact that the Abwehr, under the erratic direction of Admiral Wilhelm Canaris, was badly organised and riddled with petty jealousies. At the Hamburg Stelle (station), which was responsible for infiltrating Britain, Abwehr case officers competed shamelessly with each other to bolster the reputation of their agents and thus increase their own status. (Miller, 2004, loc. 1022)

However, it appears that the Abwehr's record keeping was second to none. Abwehr officers recorded all the minutiae of their agents' training, so that Berlin knew everything about their progress, no matter where they were taught sabotage skills. The records were sent first to local headquarters and then forwarded by radio either to Hamburg, the city responsible for all activities directed against Britain, or to the Abwehr's Berlin headquarters (Booth, 2007, loc. 1208–1215).

An entire division of the Abwehr was devoted to helping its agents get messages through, in the event that they couldn't make radio contact; such assistance was essential, as transmitting from within enemy territory was dangerous. Simple triangulation techniques could trace an agent's whereabouts, and the sight of an unauthorized aerial would alert British civilians, who were encouraged to notice anything unusual in their neighborhood. The Abwehr was allegedly also experimenting with microdots (texts or images reduced to about 1 mm in diameter). These, however, were not very useful for agents in the field, as they required specialized equipment, which would have attracted attention. The so-called letter drops via neutral countries, containing messages written in invisible ink, were a safer technique (Booth, 2007, loc. 2140–2147).

In France, the Abwehr took control of a château in La Bretonnière just outside the industrial port of Nantes. Double agent Eddie Chapman (Zigzag) arrived there in the spring of 1942 and underwent months of training. "When the agents had any special missions to accomplish, any sabotage work, any espionage," he later told MI5, "then they were periodically sent out of the country" (Booth, 2007, loc. 1608). On his first day at the château, Chapman was told that he would be given a German name. All the trainees used noms de guerre, but over the next few months, Eddie found out their real names as they often told him, or he could easily discover them (Booth, 2007, loc. 1584–1592).

It was believed that the Abwehr controlled about 1500 senior agents in Spain, spread throughout the country. "Headed by Commander Gustav Leisner, this remarkable network produced such a volume of information that some thirty-four wireless operators and ten female cipher clerks were required to handle the radio traffic" (García and West, 2011, p. 80).

SOVIET UNION

Red Army's Fourth Department

Yan Karlovich Berzin, Soviet communist politician and military intelligence officer, was head of the Red Army's Fourth Department from 1920 to 1935, and again from 1937 to 1938. It was one of the six Soviet spy agencies operating abroad; its chief rivals were the Comintern's OMS (International Liaison Department) and the overseas agents of the GPU secret police. The OMS was seen as amateurish; the GPU seemed mostly concerned with hunting enemies at home and abroad, rather than gathering serious political information. Berzin, though, excelled in this latter task (Matthews, 2019, loc. 995–996).

In November 1929, Berzin recruited Richard Sorge and sent him to Berlin along with his boss, Alexander Ulanovsky. Their contact was Konstantin Basov, one of the most experienced agent trainers of his generation. Basov's job was to orchestrate the two men's cover stories, creating new identities, making invisible their Soviet past. He had procured a Czech passport for Ulanovsky, who was to become Herr Kirschner, a businessman representing a German or European company in China. Ulanovsky had to place classified advertisements in the *Berliner Tageblatt* and the *Berliner Zeitung*, presenting himself as an independent salesman in metal, planning to move to China, thus offering his services as a trade representative.

To Basov's surprise, the Schelder-Consortium, a company based in Rotterdam specializing in the export of German arms, responded immediately, offering Kirschner the position of their official agent in China. However, arms exports from Germany to China were at the time banned by the Treaty of Versailles and the League of Nations. The Schelder-Consortium did not see it as a difficulty. In their opinion, this ban could be circumvented thanks to the company's contacts with the Belgian and French members of the Allied Commission of the Rhine, who were supposed to monitor Germany's rearmament. These corrupt officials could provide false export certificates for shipments of German arms to nonexistent customers in India and Indochina, with the weapons ultimately diverted to China. The Schelder-Consortium's proposal was clearly illegal, and as such perhaps a risky cover for an active Soviet spy. Nonetheless, Basov decided that a position as an international arms smuggler would help Ulanovsky make contacts in Chinese military circles, and the Fourth Department agreed (Matthews, 2019, loc. 1086–1093).

In September 1933, Sorge was sent to Japan to organize an intelligence network. The Fourth Department decided that Sorge should once more hide in plain sight, working as the now-respected German journalist and Asia expert. They drilled him in the latest cipher codes, based on page and line numbers of the 1933 edition of the German Statistical Yearbook. Sorge was severely warned against any contact with local Japanese communists, who were apparently infiltrated by police informers. He was also to avoid officials of the Soviet embassy in Tokyo, who were kept under constant supervision. All that remained for the Fourth Department was to equip Sorge with a fresh set of German journalistic accreditations and letters of introduction to top German and Japanese officials in Tokyo. He became the Japan correspondent for the *Frankfurter Zeitung*, which was launched in 1856 and was one of the few democratic papers in Germany in the 1920s (Matthews, 2019, loc. 1846).

Sorge's relocation to Japan in 1933 brought to light the rivalry between Soviet organizations. In Moscow, Comintern intelligence and Soviet military intelligence could operate as separate, and even rival, entities. In Shanghai and Tokyo, the lives of the different sets of Soviet spies were inextricably tangled, as they were much more visible (Matthews, 2019, loc. 1625), and conflicts intensified. Berzin appears to have been removed from his position in the spring of 1935 and, until June 1936, served as Deputy Commander of the army in the Soviet Far East. During the next year, he was Chief Military Adviser to the Republican forces in the Spanish Civil War. In June 1937, Berzin was recalled from Spain and reappointed as Head of the Fourth Department. This position ended with Berzin's arrest on May 13, 1938, during the Great Purge. On July 29, 1938, he was shot in the cellars of the Lublyanka headquarters in Moscow.[2] Apparently, working at the office could be more dangerous than working in the field, at least in the Soviet Union.

---

[2]   https://military.wikia.org/wiki/Jānis_K._Bērziņš, accessed May 24, 2021.

ISRAEL

Mossad

Mossad is the national intelligence agency of Israel, responsible for intelligence collection, covert operations, and counterterrorism. Formed in 1949 as the Central Institute for Coordination, it has been described as a "deep state," as it is exempt from the constitutional laws of the state of Israel.

Reuven Shiloah, the first Director of Mossad (1949–1952), was known for creating a Jewish brigade within the British Army during the Second World War. He was followed by Isser Harel, previously the head of Israel security agency Shin Bet. Meir Amit, Director from 1963 to 1968, introduced a serious change in priorities concerning intelligence gathering: human intelligence (HUMINT) began to be replaced by technological surveillance (signal intelligence, or SIGINT), which used strategies such as wiretapping and bugging (Bar-Joseph, 2017, p. 46).

From 1968 to 1974, Zvi Zamir—a former Major General in the Israeli Defence Forces—was Director of Mossad. When he started the job, he spent hours going over the dossier of every Mossad operative and held ongoing consultations with Rafael Eitan, the head of a branch called Tzomet—the collection department that has principal responsibility for espionage, with field officers operating under official and nonofficial cover around the world. Zamir set out to discover how sources were valued, recruited, and handled and how their potential could be maximized. He even scrutinized the files of operatives who had stopped working with the agency and, in at least one case, convinced Tzomet to reengage an agent, resulting in some high-value intelligence for Israel. Along the way, Zamir learned about the potential fragility of the relationship between a handler and his operative and the importance of the handler's ability to recognize and meet the agent's psychological needs. He also learned that money was a central—but not the sole— motive for most agents, according to Bar-Joseph (2017, p. 45).

UNITED STATES

FBI

The FBI was established in 1908 as the Bureau of Investigation (BOI); it became the Federal Bureau of Investigation (FBI) in 1935. The FBI is the domestic intelligence and security service of the United States, and its principal federal law enforcement agency. It is the leading US counterterrorism, counterintelligence criminal investigative organization, and its activities are similar to those of MI5 and the Russian FSB. At present, it maintains 56 field offices in major cities and more than 400 resident agencies in smaller cities and areas across the United States. After the death of John Edgar Hoover—the FBI's Director from 1924 to 1972—Congress passed legislation that limited the tenure of future FBI Directors to ten years.

At the end of the Second World War, Hoover had, in the words of William C. Sullivan (who later moved from the FBI to the CIA), "the entire world staked out for the FBI and had opened offices in a great many foreign capitals" (Tate, 2021, loc. 513). But when the Central Intelligence Agency (CIA) was created in 1947, it was given sole responsibility for espionage; the FBI was ordered to shut down most of its international operations and to turn over all responsibility for running foreign-based agents to the CIA.

OSS

The Office of Strategic Services (OSS, 1942–1945) was an intelligence agency of the United States during the Second World War and a predecessor of the Department of State's Bureau of Intelligence and Research, and the CIA. The OSS was created to coordinate espionage activities behind enemy lines for all branches of the US Armed Forces. Other OSS functions included propaganda, subversion, and postwar planning. The agency proved especially useful in providing a worldwide overview of the German war effort, its strengths, and weaknesses.

CIA

In July 1947, President Harry Truman decided that a single, civilian foreign intelligence organization was needed. When he signed the National

Security Act, the CIA was born, but its early years were not straightforward. Three branches of government with different priorities were to control the new agency. Truman wanted the CIA to focus on strategic information regarding enemies of the United States. The Department of Defense required military information and covert action, whereas the State Department felt that the CIA should bring about worldwide political change favorable to US interests. CIA's staff were scattered across the capital in several dilapidated offices, and communication between the operational espionage branches and the analytical counterintelligence department (the Office) was often complicated.

In 1954, President Dwight Eisenhower asked Lieutenant General James Doolittle to prepare a "Report on the Covert Activities of the Central Intelligence Agency":

> Doolittle concluded by recommending a wholesale reorganization of the CIA and the streamlining of its operations—not least by bringing its various branches, then housed in forty-three different buildings, scattered across Washington DC, under one roof. The costs of constructing what would eventually become its Langley headquarters in Virginia would be vast—but then money was not one of the Agency's many problems. (Tate, 2021, loc. 686)

For more than a decade, the FBI and the CIA had been locked in a turf war over intelligence. According to the law, the CIA was forbidden from operating inside US borders, as domestic security and counterespionage were the FBI's domains. Yet, the FBI could, and at times did, carry out secret activities overseas, while the CIA has had a limited domestic function. The conflicts were unavoidable, but, as the history of other intelligence offices shows, not exceptional.[3]

In 1954, James Jesus Angleton was made chief of counterintelligence for the CIA. He became famous, among other reasons, for favoring some defectors and ignoring others; Tate (2021) described Angleton's ignorance of exceptionally valuable information provided by the Polish defector Michał Goleniewski. Angleton remained a controversial figure, and he "was forced out of the CIA in 1974, when the extent of his illegal mole-hunting was revealed. He retired with his orchids, his fishing rods and his secrets, a man of deep and enduring mystery, and a brilliant fool" (Macintyre, 2014, p. 281). Aside from the Goleniewski affair, Angleton

---

[3]   https://www.nbcnews.com/id/wbna6973534, accessed September 5, 2022.

also placed his trust in Philby, right up until the latter's defection to the Soviet Union in 1963 (Hanning, 2021).

Amy B. Zegart described the history of the CIA (and other US national security agencies) and has not been impressed by its development. In her opinion, "the CIA has proved remarkably resistant to the force of events" (1999, p. 222), and its original problems remained. The world kept changing, but the CIA has not initiated any major shifts in its mission, design, or operations. Zegart concluded that this was partly due to the CIA's "schizophrenic" character (p. 11). Zegart referred to the CIA's coordinating/analysis unit, and operational branches, which had two kinds of operations: covert intelligence collection and covert action. Because of the aforementioned bureaucratic conflicts at the point of its design, the CIA's analytical counterintelligence department, that is, the Office, has floundered: "CIA design reflected the interests and desires of existing intelligence organizations—the very actors who most wanted it to fail" (Zegart, 1999, p. 188).

The terrorist attacks of September 11, 2001, changed everything: "In the wake of the attack, the intelligence community mobilized with one overriding goal: preventing another 9/11. The CIA, the National Security Agency, and the 15 other components of the US intelligence community restructured, reformed, and retooled. Congress appropriated billions of dollars to support the transformation" (Zegart and Morell, 2019).

In the years that followed, the CIA extended its activities to offensive cyber-operations. These were successful, but Amy Zegart and Michael Morell (in 2019 acting director of the CIA) warned that it might not be enough:

> ...today, confronted with new threats that go well beyond terrorism, U.S. intel-ligence agencies face another moment of reckoning. From biotechnology and nanotechnology to quantum computing and artificial intelligence (AI), rapid technological change is giving U.S. adversaries new capabilities and eroding traditional U.S. intelligence advantages. The U.S. intelligence community must adapt to these shifts or risk failure as the nation's first line of defense. (ibid.)

The authors had no doubt, however, that the CIA is at present perceived as a monolithic organization, in spite of the variety of its activities.

In general, developments in the offices of secret service organizations showed strong similarities to those in standard organizations, which is somewhat surprising, considering how dangerous "standard" conflicts and competition could turn out to be in the context of intelligence agencies. Perhaps the rules of bureaucracy are stronger and more pervasive than one might expect.

5. Training

Learning is the process by which a person acquires new knowledge, skills, and capabilities. Training, in turn, involves systematic and planned instruction and development activities (Armstrong, 2003). So, how do secret agents learn their profession? The review of spy autobiographies and biographies suggests that they learn on the job, but thorough training is essential.

We begin with some detailed description of training in Poland based on the autobiography of an intelligence officer who between 1977 and 1979 underwent such training, which seemed to incorporate the basic skills for agents. We learned from our material that these skills were recognized by practically all intelligence agencies.[1] Then, we present specific skills and the changing ways of teaching them owing to developing technology and geopolitical situations. It should be added that, at certain times and in particular countries (e.g., Sweden), intelligence organizations, especially those belonging to the army, did not train women (Guillou, 2019–2020).

WHAT AN "ORDINARY SPY" NEEDS TO KNOW

Filip Hagenbeck, a Polish intelligence officer, wrote about his time as "an ordinary spy" between 1979 and 1990 (*Zwyczajny szpieg*, 2019). He described the training for candidates at the Ministry of Interior Affairs (Ministerstwo Spraw Wewnętrznych in Polish). The process began with a meeting with the High Qualification Commission, during which, apart from answering questions and receiving instructions, the candidate was to choose his future "legalization name." The next part of the process was what Hagenbeck called "purgatory" (suggesting that a hell was to follow): monthly military preparation in a small town near Warsaw. Hagenbeck had already completed his military service, but several other

---

[1]   Allegedly, new entrants to MI5 had no formal training: just a ten-day immersion in the exercise of "staff duties." This informality was explained by the fact that "the technical experts within MI5 tended to be mavericks, disdainful of the rules" (Sisman, 2015, pp. 189–190).

candidates had for different reasons been released from compulsory service, therefore everyone (there were 55 men in the group) had to undergo the training.

The next stage took place at the Intelligence Personnel Training Center, located in a restricted military area in a forest near Stare Kiejkuty. The Center served until 1989 as the only intelligence training facility in the Eastern Bloc located outside the Soviet Union (Severski, 2015).

Personnel management textbooks (e.g., Armstrong, 2003) suggest that the key to effective training is the creation of a positive learning environment, which stresses the importance of encouragement and support, as well as good facilities. The complex at Stare Kiejkuty had a lake, swimming pool, sauna, and heliport, along with tennis, volleyball, and basketball courts. Trainees with families lived apart from the other trainees, so that family members would not remember too many faces; others slept in the dormitory. Most were young men, but there were also "uncles," and one "grandfather" (a man with gray hair).

Sundays were free, but the rest of the week began every day at 06.00 with a morning assembly in the square in front of the dormitory, followed by a morning run. Afterward, there were classes in languages and political science. Trainees were divided into teams according to their language and level of knowledge. It was assumed, not always correctly, that a language could always be learned and improved. The political science classes focused on the functioning of the North Atlantic Treaty Organization and the European Economic Community. Trainees learned to work with intelligence information; in the end, they had to write a thesis.

In operational classes, trainees typically practiced "operational conversations"—with "white noise," best produced in the toilets by flushing. One of the most important lessons was how to walk and move under the eyes of counterintelligence, carried out with the help of "test routes"; the trainee had to decide whether he was being watched, and then perform his task or refuse it and connect with his so-called personal source. After completing the route, if the trainee falsely claimed that he was being followed, he was considered a "ghost hunter" and could be considered incapable of operational work.

Trainees also learned to recognize areas in which monitors and cameras were located, although there were far fewer of these in the 1970s. They were taught to lead observers from counterintelligence to a place where the observers could be lost. Therefore, the "test routes" were never used by the persons who designed them as the "counterintelligence" may have noticed that they were exploring the area. The trick was to lead the "tail" in a way that would reveal the person tailing you.

The role of observers was played by specialist colleagues from the B Office of the Military Intelligence Agency. Trainees were told to pay special attention to the observers' footwear, as the observation crew usually had a wardrobe in the car and changed clothes without changing shoes. No vehicles were used in training—perhaps because of insufficient funds to acquire them, but the official explanation was that it was easier to recognize an observer if he or she was forced to walk.

Observation skills were also tested in various provincial cities on established test routes, which were divided into separate sections. At the end of each section was a "Time Control Point," including intelligence tasks such as the "Rapid Transfer of Material" to another officer, in front of the observers.

Then there was a "next conversation": a meeting with an operational contact or agent who had already been recruited. The candidate received intelligence information from an agent who pretended to be an experienced officer; the candidate was to verify the truthfulness of the source, asking about facts that he had already gleaned from the case file, but not . directly from the agent. Then the candidate was required to validate the usefulness of the established communication system by analyzing the source's personal situation; if necessary, change the system, and arrange another meeting. Then they both wrote reports.

There was also training in "defrosting conversations." In this, a person pretended to be an agent who was "frozen," which meant that cooperation with him or her was suspended for some reason. After some time, such an agent stopped appearing even for control meetings (during which the runner only checked if the agent was alive and well). If the agent did not appear for a long time, at the next defrosting meeting the trainee's task was to establish the "real" motives of the agent's behavior and plan further actions.

In the afternoons, there were three-hour language laboratories, using the then popular German UHER tape recorders. Trainees were given short texts that had to be retold in their own words. They also tried to listen to the BBC and Radio Liberty, but the language in these programs was too complicated, so they switched to "Broadcast in Special English."

Hagenbeck liked the photography classes, because, for a social scientist, they felt exotic. Candidates were also shown a "museum" of spy gadgets and were taught to encrypt texts, with the help of combination codes and other such devices.

Then there were "swallows," simulated diplomatic meetings, during which trainees were monitored for how much they could drink without getting drunk. Also, Hagenbeck believed that bromide was added to their tea to suppress their sex drive.

They were all assigned "carers," officers who were experienced in working abroad. However, some intelligence officers were not sent to the training center, but directly to an "external position" within the target organization or to an intermediate "cover-up job." Such candidates were prepared for service individually, and they were instructed to avoid contact with the office, except for their controller. These candidates were called "second-line officers." Still others were sent to perform illegal services; they were exported abroad on false documents and were dormant for a long time. Hagenbeck felt this was preparation for the next potential war, which would prevent normal consular and diplomatic relations.

Hagenbeck concluded as follows:

> Being a spy, even so "ordinary," requires many skills. The adepts acquire a set of such skills, essential for the intelligence craft, during basic training and the first years of service at the Office. But in this profession, other skills are also desirable, not spy-like at all. From the very first days of training, our supervisors, as well as other lecturers and guests arriving at Kiejkuty emphasized that every spy, even the ordinary one, must be "extraordinary" in some aspect. He or she must be interesting for people around them, which is especially important when working in the field abroad. (2019, p. 127, transl. BC)

Yet, the title of Hagenbeck's book was precisely "an ordinary spy". a meta-joke, or an admission of his own unsuitability?

A VARIETY OF SKILLS—ACROSS TIME AND PLACE

Coding and Decoding

Spies working for the Abwehr during the Second World War were subjected to training similar to an academic course of study, including some special skills. Potential German spies were usually taught Morse code, radio transmissions, the use of ciphers and invisible inks, basic countersurveillance techniques, and the recognition of aircraft types (Booth, 2007, loc. 1769).

> Hauptmann Bruhns (…) gave short courses on military matters, such as the equipment which the British Army and Air Force used, their airports, anti-aircraft artillery, camouflage, map reading, and he was also their teacher in meteorology. He explained that the information from Britain which the Abwehr were most interested in was the location of new airbases, what sort of defences they were equipped with, roads, radio communications, staffing, equipment, data on aircraft types, and number of aircraft. (Jonason and Olsson, 2011, pp. 8–9)

For example, British double agent Eddie Chapman (Zigzag) was, in 1942, taken by the Germans to a château at St Joseph by the Loire. There, he was assigned training officers "who would, in the months ahead, teach him all he would ever need to know about the use of radio transmissions and sabotage" (Booth, 2007, loc. 1215). One officer had the job of teaching Chapman the "black arts" of the Morse code. They began by using a simple wireless: it had a battery, a tapping key, and headphones. Chapman was so talented that often the operators would ask him to practice in the Radio Room, from where all the official radio communications were transmitted.

Using a simple numerical code, Chapman practiced transmissions twice a day, sending to Paris at 10 a.m. and to Bordeaux an hour later. Also, his linguistic skills turned out to be of use: in the beginning he used English or French, but later he sent messages in German as not all the operators were bilingual (Booth, 2007).

As well as learning the fundamentals of Morse code, Chapman was also taught elementary radio shorthand and the practical skills of constructing a radio (Macintyre, 2007).

Harry Williamson (Tate), another double agent working for the Allies and Germany, was trained by the Germans in Morse telegraphy, enabling him to send 100 characters and receive 80 characters per minute (a qualified telegraphist managed to send at least 130 characters per minute). He also received tuition in radio equipment (Jonason and Olsson, 2011).

Mossad's agent, the Egyptian Ashraf Marwan (the Angel) took on the role of an "alarm agent," who could give a real-time warning if the Egyptians were about to attack. Mossad sent an expert to London, where Marwan was staying, to give him a crash course in using a wireless device. How to hide the device was also explained, and Marwan was equipped with a list of frequencies. However, as a Mossad agent remarked, Marwan had "two left hands" (Bar-Joseph, 2017, p. 127) and he wasn't very good with gadgets. At the next meeting with his handlers, Marwan told them that it was just too dangerous and that he had tossed the device into the river. "In all his years working for the Mossad, the greatest spy in Israel's history never once passed information via wireless communication" (ibid.).

In a similar vein, the double agent Dušan Popov (Tricycle) was given a Leica camera by his Abwehr handler, who also taught him how to use it, but Popov never learned to develop his own pictures (Miller, 2004, loc. 688).

Shooting, Knifing, and Exploding

One aspect of Chapman's training made it clear that, in the event of finding himself in a difficult situation, he would be expected to shoot his way out of trouble. Luckily, he "excelled at marksmanship, particularly in shooting liqueur glasses in a row or coins in a bulls-eye from fifteen metres' distance" (Booth, 2007, loc. 1854).

He was also taught to use explosives by a professional chemist: "Every day, Chapman and Wojch [his tutor] would work in the laboratory, making homemade bombs and incendiary devices from simple ingredients such as sugar, oil and potassium chlorate. Chapman was set to work memorizing formulae" (Macintyre, 2007, pp. 51–52).

He was taught how to attach wires to an ordinary wristwatch, in order to create a timer for up to twelve hours (longer delays required an alarm clock). His tutor showed him the best place to destroy a bridge, how to set explosives to wreck trains by putting charges on railway lines, and how to put sand in engines. He also learned the art of concealing explosive devices in attaché cases, packing clothes to muffle an alarm clock inside a suitcase, and making a bomb by drilling a piece of coal and filling it with dynamite (Booth, 2007).

Chapman even learned how to construct a booby trap from a package that exploded when the string around it was cut (Macintyre, 2007). Sent to Norway, he learned new, "more advanced ways of causing explosions with limpets, magnetic clams, detonators—including a new process he had not been aware of, involving explosive pellets dried in a muslin sleeve" (Booth, 2007, loc. 420).

The training at SIS (MI6) in the 1950s included marksmanship and the use of a knife. At Fort Monckton, the secret service training base in Hampshire, David Cornwell (le Carré) and his fellow trainees fired 9 mm automatic pistols at life-size pop-up targets and were taught knife fighting by an instructor who had previously worked in the Shanghai police. During lessons in unarmed combat, they were shown target areas of the body, and learned how to kill a person with a single blow. They climbed telegraph poles and detonated explosives in the moat of the Fort. At night they were taken by Royal Navy motor torpedo boats to practice landing agents on and evacuating them from a hostile coastline (Sisman, 2015).

Parachuting and Getting Out of the Sea

Using a parachute was an important skill, fraught with danger for the novice, but taught in a more rudimentary way by the Germans. Chapman learned to parachute using a ladder propped against a tree in the garden; a Luftwaffe officer taught him how to avoid injury by rolling when landing (Booth, 2007). Prior to joining MI5, in 1950 Cornwell attended a short parachute course at RAF Abingdon, in which he jumped from a tethered balloon (Sisman, 2015).

Most likely, the women agents under the supervision of Vera Atkins were also taught how to parachute, but Stevenson (2011) emphasized the exercise of escaping from downed planes—involving the necessary repetition of a particular exercise or learned skill to foster a sense of emotional detachment, crucial for spies in the Second World War.

> He [a naval pilot] prompted [Vera Atkins] to make use of downed airmen, who covered the length and breadth of France, which was how she now came to be standing in rain puddles in the gloom while pilots timed each other's exits from the cockpits of the four silent Hellcats as if trapped upside-down under the sea. They endlessly repeated a tiresome routine: release links to the cockpit, kick off boots, loosen clothing, suck in air trapped in the canopy while the machine sinks into cold black terrors. No panic. Mind separated from body. (...) The loss of such men led to their successors drilling each other in this boring procedure. They lightened it by competing to beat each other's escape timings. (2011, p. 245)

Meteorology and Geography

During his career as a British double agent, Williamson was required to send weather reports to the Abwehr, and more than half of his reports concerned meteorological data. The weather was fundamental to all air and navy operations.

> Already during his training in Hamburg, the Germans had pointed out the importance of weather reports and that he should send them as often as possible, preferably every day. This instruction was given to most of the Abwehr agents sent to Great Britain. The weather forecast was, for example, of major importance to those controlling German night fighters in their desperate combat against the Allied bomber armadas over Germany. (Jonason and Olsson, 2011, pp. 111–112)

Geographical knowledge was important because double agents needed to live a life as close as possible to the one they were pretending to live. "If, say, the double agent was claiming to transmit from Aylesbury, then he needed to know what Aylesbury was like and, if possible, to be physically in or very near Aylesbury, since it was suspected that the Germans could pinpoint transmissions, perhaps to within a one-mile radius" (Macintyre, 2007, pp. 71–72).

When Chapman was sent by the Germans to England to sabotage the De Havilland aircraft factory, he started preparations for readapting to a country from which he had been absent for three years. He listened to the BBC and read English newspapers, along with a London guidebook to recall street locations (Macintyre, 2007).

Writing

Writing reports constitutes a significant part of a spy's activities—they are an important tool in deception as well as in providing information. As the Polish agent Severski (2015) claimed, espionage is writing, continuous writing, which is why spies receive instruction:

> The most rigorous instruction in prose writing that I ever received came, not from any schoolteacher or university tutor, least of all from a writing school. It came from the classically educated senior officers on the top floor of MI5's headquarters in Curzon Street, Mayfair, who seized on my reports with gleeful pedantry, heaping contempt on my dangling clauses and gratuitous adverbs, scoring the margins of my deathless prose with such comments as redundant–omit–justify–sloppy–do you really mean this? No editor I have since encountered was so exacting, or so right. (le Carré, 2016, p. 21)

Perhaps this is why so many ex-agents have described their experiences in books—fiction and autobiographies—written by themselves or with the help of a professional writer. Nigel West, for instance, edited Guy Liddell's diaries as well as co-authoring Juan Pujol García's (Garbo) autobiography.

Learning the Cover Job

Filip Hagenbeck ("an ordinary spy") pointed out that an officer appointed to work in a foreign residency must undergo two preparation courses: one at the office and the other in the organization that serves as a cover. In his case, the latter was the Consular Department of the Ministry of Foreign Affairs, where the requirements for cover persons were higher than those for regular employees:

> Colleagues leaving for diplomatic posts dealing with economic, political or press matters did not have to take difficult consular examinations. Also, my colleagues who were sent to consulates in Washington, Chicago, London, Montreal, Paris or Bonn, where the staff had their specialties, had to pass exams only in their specialization—passport, legal-succession, legalization, i.e., authentication of various documents, including marital status, or visa. I [going to Lagos] had no one to help and had to pass all the exams. (Hagenbeck, 2019, p. 353, transl. BC)

SURVIVAL SKILLS

Physical Challenges

Obviously, survival skills were important during the Second World War. Thus, to make sure that SOE training met the expectations of their trainers, Vera Atkins

> … revisited the rugged terrain at Loch Ailort, twenty-four miles west of Fort William on the coast of Scotland, where young men and women lived in a grim old house with cold granite walls, whipped constantly by high winds, that was hardly ever visible through the thick tall trees reaching higher than the roof. Mist and rain soaked the surrounding hills. The region was gloomy beyond belief, and the high fatality rate among aircrews at a nearby naval air station was almost entirely due to pilots flying into hilltops or losing their way in foul weather and running out of fuel far out to sea. (Stevenson, 2011, p. 197)

The idea was to prepare the agents for survival in places such as Soviet labor camps in Siberia. And the psychological challenges were perhaps more difficult to handle than the physical threats. As Polish intelligence officer Severski said in an interview: "The officer must be perceptive, have the ability to observe, analyze the environment, and have strong legs, good stomach, strong nerves, and memory."[2]

Psychological Challenges

> Espionage is the art of lying. We call it legending. We must be able to lie in the highest form, which is manipulating people. (...) it is just a work tool, one of many. We only legend for business purposes. The spy does not lie or cheat privately—why would he do that? Contrary to popular belief, an intelligence officer is a profession for people with a high sense of ethics, but also a good knowledge of life. (ibid.)

Severski stressed the importance of perceptiveness enhanced by the ability to quickly analyze facts and draw conclusions. Some qualities are innate—if, for example, during an observation exercise,

> ...someone sees ghosts, it means they are panicking. And in a spy's life, panic is worse than carelessness. Of course, we try to teach young spies so that they can manage panic, but without a gift from nature, it can't be learned. This gift alone is not enough. An officer, as he walks on the test route, which is the basis of our work, can only look back once, because if he does it twice, he will be unmasked .... (ibid.)

Safety and self-preservation are significantly enhanced by strong observational skills, but not descending into panic can often be the difference between success and failure for a spy.

> Try standing alone on the streets of New York, stony-broke. You've tapped whoever you can tap, milked your contacts dry. In England you're on the Wanted list, and you're on the Wanted list here in New York. You daren't show your passport, you're using false names to hop between apartments you can't pay for, and all that stands between you and perdition is your animal wit and a double-breasted pinstripe from Berman of Savile Row that you home-press every evening. It's the kind of situation they dream up for you at spy school: "Now let's see how you talk your way out of this one." (le Carré, 2016, p. 286)

---

[2]   http://kulturalnikpoznanski.blogspot.com/2015/08/czasami-zwykle-metody-sa-najlepsze.html, accessed August 30, 2015, transl. BC.

Testing

It was widely agreed by authors that testing is a crucial element of training. In Chapman's case, testing by the Abwehr consisted principally of monitoring his practical skills, such as operating the wireless, successfully using sabotage and espionage techniques, and parachuting (Booth, 2007). It was also made clear that if Chapman passed tests, he would be sent to Britain on a mission and, if successful, would be rewarded. But there was no explanation of what would happen if he failed these tests (Macintyre, 2007). After the mission, Chapman was rigorously debriefed by the Germans, who "repeatedly asked him to retell his exploits in England, alert for any logical inconsistencies" (Booth, 2007, loc. 3313). Accordingly, the British prepared him for such testing:

> Hour after hour, day after day, Chapman was coached on every detail of the tale he must tell the Germans [...] After a week of this, a Field Security Policeman named Hale was brought in to play the part of a German interrogator: he aggressively pummeled Chapman with questions: where had he lived, who had he seen, how had he obtained explosives, and what had he discovered? (Macintyre, 2007, pp. 182–183)

Popov underwent similar intensive testing by German and English interrogators. His debriefing

> ... by Major Robertson and three other MI5 officers took place in French, a language in which he was more comfortable than English, and continued for four days without interruption. The questioning was merciless as his interrogators probed for any inconsistency that would indicate he was lying. He was made to go over his story time and time again. (Miller, 2004, loc 146)

When Popov returned to Lisbon, his German runner repeated the performance, questioning him closely about every detail of his report, asking about the places in Britain that he had visited, and the sources for his hearsay information (Miller, 2004, loc 146).

Spymistress Vera Atkins's biographer related an instance of extreme testing:

> Tied to the railway tracks was a blindfolded girl, Rolande Colas (...). She was back from a brief mission in France and was taking special training to deal with dangers she understood firsthand, but for which few trainee agents were fully prepared. For this exercise, she was told to guard a piece of information with her life. She was told a train would thunder through within five

minutes. She still had time to confess. Vera, playing her conducting officer, said to the training sergeant, within the girl's hearing, "Switch the points, Sarge. I hear the train coming!" "Yes, ma'am. Pass me the lever." "I gave it to you!" "You've got it, ma'am!" "Oh shit! Where is it?" The noise of the train reverberated. Vera shouted, "Cut the girl free!" "Too late, ma'am. Jump clear!" Rolande stayed silent. The train passed on the other track. (Stevenson, 2011, p. 136)

Luckily, not all testing was so dramatic. When Cornwell (le Carré) was being trained by the SIS in the 1950s, some exercises descended into farce:

> The point of one exercise was to kidnap an MI6 officer disguised as a passing cyclist and subject him to mock torture; unfortunately, they chose the wrong cyclist, an innocent schoolmaster. As the climax to a map-reading exercise, a low-flying RAF aircraft was supposed to drop a wireless set by parachute. The young men below waited in eager anticipation as the parcel drifted to earth; but when they retrieved and unwrapped it, they were disappointed to find that their masters had not risked a precious piece of equipment on a mere training exercise. "It's full of fucking stones!" (Sisman, 2015, p. 212)

On another exercise, each of the trainees had to retrieve a cache of arms buried somewhere in the forest; Cornwell's had been concealed at a spot occupied by a large car with a pair of dozing tourists inside. It needed all his charm to persuade the couple to move on so that he could begin digging. When he was required to act as a German tourist in Brighton, he met his wife's aunt on the street. On the final day of this exercise, the local police, instructed by SIS, arrested him and subjected him to an intense interrogation to test whether he could maintain his cover under pressure. Apparently, Cornwell managed to speak with a convincing German accent.

In London, the SIS trainees learned about the psychology of traitors, double agents, and defectors, and how to obtain, motivate, and control them. They were shown how to forge papers, make skeleton keys, pick locks, and operate secret electronic equipment. They practiced taking photographs from cameras concealed in special briefcases and learned how to develop films. The skills of spies were truly impressive.

Secrecy

The requirement for secrecy would be better described as a legal demand than a skill. For example, everyone who worked at Bletchley Park—the principal center of Allied codebreaking during the Second World War—had to sign the Official Secrets Act (Grey, 2012). However, instructions concerning secrecy were also given to the general public ("careless talk costs lives"), and there were those specific to organizations, not just the secret service ("need to know"[3]), which survive until today. As Costas and Grey rightly observed, "[S]ecrecy is endemic within work organizations" (2016, p. 1). What is especially interesting is the accompanying lack of curiosity, as described by Grey: "The acquired habit of 'not telling' was in Bletchley soon supplemented by 'not asking'" (2012, p. 24).

In secret service organizations, the "legends"—fake profiles—helped to keep secret the agents' activities while permitting them to participate in everyday interactions, giving plausible explanations when asked. As Costas and Grey (2016) pointed out, keeping secrets is a matter of disciplining oneself, of controlling both emotions and expressions. Standard organizations, especially those producing new technologies, also have high secrecy requirements, but they do not relate to private life, like in secret service organizations. Still, the industrial espionage agents (usually employed by standard organizations, and acting illegally) may be trained in a similar manner to the secret service agents.

---

[3]   Catino calls it "compartmentation" (2019, p. 268), but his approach is structuralist, whereas ours is processual, which is more appropriate for secret service organizations, where "the need to know" varies from one issue to another, and from time to time.

6. Line management

The approach to line management changes according to managerial fads and fashions, not least when it concerns personnel management. In recent management literature, it has been accepted that personnel managers in standard organizations do not usurp line managers' roles but are there to support them in "getting things done through people" (Armstrong, 2003, p. 43). So, how do line managers get things done through secret agents?

Line management in intelligence work takes place on several stages. The first and most important is the running of agents by controllers, runners, handlers, protectors, or case officers in the office: "It is well known that the early relationship between a handler and his agent can have a huge impact on the source's long-term ability to contribute" (Bar-Joseph, 2017, p. 42). Bar-Joseph continued, "A successful handler combined a variety of outstanding skills and traits. John le Carré, who served in British intelligence, once described the successful handler as offering his operative an 'image of mentor, shepherd, parent and befriender, as prop and marriage counselor, as pardoner, entertainer, and protector ...'" (2017, p. 52).

Second, there is what might be called "impression management,"[1] a form of self-management: what the agents permit (or do not permit) themselves to do, and how. It is a kind of projection of a personal image to the environment.

The third concerns the construction of a network of subagents, which can be carried out by the office by sending a ready-made network to be managed by the agent in the field; alternatively, subagents are recruited by the agents themselves and managed accordingly. The fourth element of line management is the recruitment and management of informants, both planned and accidental. Those considered to be especially trustworthy and promising can become subagents and join the network.

---

[1]   In his book *Strategic Interaction* (1970), Erving Goffman, who coined the term, paid much attention to spies and their interactions.

The means and the methods of line management in intelligence work are partly standard and partly unique. But even a largely successful management can end in failure, caused by circumstances or by the agent's mistake. In such cases, compatriot agents with an official position in another country (e.g., as embassy employees) could be simply recalled home. This was not always straightforward, and in certain cases foreign agents had to be exfiltrated, usually via neutral countries. The exfiltration of Guy Burgess, Donald Maclean, and Kim Philby, members of the so-called Cambridge Five spy ring, has been described by many authors (see, e.g., Macintyre, 2014; Hanning, 2021).

The methods of line management, though with many similarities among different secret service organizations, changed with time and across different countries (not only due to changes in technology, but also because of political situations).

1919–1938

Soviet Union

Running agents
The handlers of Richard Sorge, "Stalin's master agent" (Matthews, 2019), changed constantly, as events in the Soviet Union, even those concerning the Red Army's Fourth Department (which employed Sorge), were even more dramatic than in Japan, where Sorge worked. Their handling more often created problems than offered solutions—problems that Sorge had to solve himself. For example, his handlers selected and sent to Japan members of the network that Sorge was supposed to run, without consulting him.

> With the arrival of Wendt, Vukelić and Miyagi, Sorge's network was, in theory, ready to start its covert work. In practice, however, the cadres that Centre [the office] had hastily, and apparently randomly, selected for the rezidentura were proving useless. By spring, Wendt had assembled his transmitter in the attic of his house in Yokohama and successfully made contact with the powerful Soviet military radios of "Weisbaden" (Vladivostok). But though the radio man was supposedly under less scrutiny than Sorge was in Tokyo, Wendt clearly lacked his boss's iron nerve. Even when he did pluck up the courage to communicate with Centre, Wendt's transmissions were often incomplete. [He] "drank all the time and often neglected to send out the information," wrote Sorge. "Spying work must be done bravely. He was cowardly." (Matthews, 2019, loc. 2458)

Matthews added that "Miyagi was also proving anything but a natural-born spy. He had come to Japan under the impression that his help was required to set up a Comintern group of idealistic Japanese socialists, not to act as a secret agent" (2019, loc. 2464–5).

Sorge used his charisma to persuade Miyagi Yotoku to take his role as planned, but Wendt still did not work effectively. The main medium of communication with Moscow was microfilm, transported via Shanghai by the otherwise useless Vukelić. "But beyond the Fourth Department's poor choice of radio man, Sorge's own planning had been meticulous" (Matthews, 2019, loc. 2631).

Impression management
Even managing himself could be a problem for Sorge, especially when drinking and riding his motorcycle, although when it came to the tasks that truly mattered, Sorge was unparalleled. Arriving in Tokyo, where he stayed for almost a decade, Sorge chose a place to stay that seemed ill-suited for a spy, as it could be entered from three directions, one of which was in the vicinity of a police station. There was no way to access his accommodation without being seen by the neighbors, and that was the point—hiding in plain sight. He used similar tactics in his observable behavior, never making any attempt to conceal his unorthodox views, often expressing his admiration for the Red Army and for Stalin. As Matthews put it, "Sorge was adept at using honesty—or an appearance of honesty—as a species of camouflage" (2019, loc. 2413).

> Sorge himself understood that his peers saw him as "a slightly lazy, high-living reporter." That was, indeed, part of Sorge's true nature. But it was also his cover. Some, in hindsight, saw through the false ingenuousness of Sorge's lovable, louche alcoholic act. It was "a calculated part of his masquerade," American reporter Joseph Newman of the *New York Herald Tribune* wrote later. "He created the impression of being a playboy, almost a wastrel, the very antithesis of a keen and dangerous spy." (Matthews, 2019, loc. 2417)

Network management
After Sorge convinced Miyagi that his task was to spy and not create a Comintern group (which took him five meetings to accomplish), they started to construct an alternative network to that selected by the Fourth Department. Miyagi went to Shanghai to contact Sorge's collaborator from his stay there, Ozaki Hotsumi, who worked at a big Japanese law firm. Ozaki discovered Sorge's real name only two years later; before that, he believed Sorge was a US journalist called Johnson.

Sorge asked Ozaki to collect information for the Comintern, just as Sorge was doing in Shanghai.

> Ozaki, by his own account, readily agreed without qualm. "I made up my mind to do spy activity with Sorge again. I accepted his request readily, and since then up to the time of my arrest I have been engaged in espionage activity," Ozaki would later tell his interrogators. After the war Ozaki was to become a hero for Japanese leftists as a true patriot who put his conscience before blind obedience to his country. (Matthews, 2019, loc. 2492)

From Sorge's point of view, this remake of his network was an improvement on its previous incarnation in Shanghai, characterized by "the chaotic arrangements" made by his runners.

> All the elements that would make Sorge's spy ring the greatest such espionage network of the age—Ozaki's contacts among the Japanese elite, Sorge's access to the secret Japanese military documents the army shared with Ott [his German contact], Miyagi's assiduous groundwork—were in place. More impressively still, every piece of information that passed back and forth served to buoy the reputations of Ott, Sorge and Ozaki in the eyes of their respective superiors. Information was power, not just to governments but to all the principals of the spy ring, both witting and unwitting. (Matthews, 2019, loc. 3100)

In Tokyo, he "was able to operate freely without any compromising entanglements with local communists, uncontrollable left-wing foreign celebrities, and most importantly bumbling Comintern cadres" (Matthews, 2019, loc. 2631). The danger of such entanglements was illustrated by an event in February 1935, when the Danish police arrested in Copenhagen practically the whole Soviet network, run by Sorge's previous boss, Alexander Ulanovsky. The latter ignored instructions from Moscow and recruited local communists, one of whom was a police informer.

Informer management
Sorge did not so much steal secrets as trade them. What he learned from Ozaki, as well as news collected from British and French journalists by

Branko Vukelić, Sorge shared with the German Embassy via Eugen Ott. In return, Sorge told Ozaki what he learned at the German Embassy.

> In the wake of the Marco Polo Bridge incident,[2] Ambassador Dirksen had formed a "study group" composed of Ott, Sorge and deputy military attaché Major Erwin Scholl to analyse the escalating war in China. Their focus was on gathering information on Japan's armed forces and their deployments. Sorge's official inclusion into the embassy's innermost circle—one that handled the most urgent and sensitive secrets—took his relationship with the German state to a new level. Ott could share all the private information he liked over breakfast or drinks with his personal friend, the journalist Sorge. But including Sorge in formal, classified meetings made him something very close to an official member of Germany's intelligence establishment. (Matthews, 2019, loc. 3613).

Apart from this trading with the German Embassy and Japanese journalists, both Sorge and Miyagi recruited—on a temporary or longer-term basis—a variety of informers. For example, when the Fourth Department demanded that Sorge find some serving Japanese officers to work for the spy ring, Miyagi contacted an old acquaintance, a fellow Okinawan and socialist named Koshiro Yoshinobu (Kodai) with whom he had studied at Meiji University. When contacted by Miyagi in March 1939, Kodai was a corporal with the army reserves, working in a paper shop.

> "If a war should break out between Russia and Japan it would mean a great sacrifice not only on the part of the farmers and labourers of both countries but also on the part of the whole Japanese people," Miyagi told Kodai at their first meeting. "To avoid such a tragedy ... I am sending various data on the situation in Japan to the Comintern." (Matthews, 2019, loc. 3927)

Kodai agreed, even refusing payment for his services. Unlike Sorge, whose "booze-fueled charm," as Matthews called it, made people either love or hate him, Miyagi fitted quietly into any company, could hang out in bars, and engage strangers in easy conversation. In fact, Miyagi

---

[2]   The Marco Polo Bridge Incident, also known as the Lugou Bridge Incident or the Double-Seven Incident, was a July 1937 battle between China's National Revolutionary Army and the Imperial Japanese Army.

complained to Sorge about the time he had to spend drinking, an aspect of the job that Sorge took to easily.

> The mechanism at work seems to have been much the same for both [Kim Philby and Richard Sorge]: beginning by finding that alcohol is instant friendship, and a bar the ideal place to elicit information—and discovering, as many a drunkard has, that booze offers a respite from nagging fear—the two spies went on to court attention by their conduct, thinking no one would guess that ostentation is a kind of camouflage. (Matthews, 2019, loc. 3576)

Miyagi had also noticed that a remarkable amount of sensitive intelligence was available in the public realm, if one knew where to look (the foreign journalists usually did). Two years after arriving in Tokyo, this naive, idealistic artist controlled a network of friends, paid agents, collaborators, and unwitting fools who reported from across all of Japan.

1939–1954

Soviet Union

Running agents
It appears that double agent Kim Philby was very close to Arnold Deutsch, his Soviet controller. "'I sometimes felt we had been friends since childhood,' [Philby] wrote. 'I was certain that my life and myself interested him not so much professionally as on a human level'" (Macintyre, 2014, p. 42). For his part, Deutsch made a careful study of Philby, diagnosing insecurity beneath his dashing exterior, and a tendency to stammer.

But the actual running was done by Theodore Maly, a Hungarian former monk, who, as an army chaplain during the First World War, had been taken prisoner in the Carpathian Mountains, where he witnessed such appalling horrors that he became a revolutionary. He shared Deutsch's appreciation of Philby, and the feeling was reciprocated: Philby considered him to be intelligent and experienced.

Later, one after another the intelligence officers were declared enemies of the people by the Stalin regime, and sent to the Gulag[3] or executed. "Philby knew they were nothing of the sort. He had revered them for

---

[3]   The government agency in charge of the Soviet network of labor camps which were set up by order of Lenin, reaching its peak during Stalin's rule from the 1930s to the early 1950s. https://en.wikipedia.org/wiki/Gulag, accessed December 6, 2022.

their 'infinite patience' and 'intelligent understanding,' their 'painstaking advice, admonition and encouragement.' But in later life, he expressed little sadness over the murder of these 'marvellous men,' and offered no criticism of the tyranny that killed them" (Macintyre, 2014, p. 48).

United Kingdom, MI5

Running agents

After his training, David Cornwell (le Carré) was made a field security officer, to work in the Palais Meran, a villa on the outskirts of Graz, Austria. One of his tasks was to analyze transcriptions of intercepted telephone calls; another to interrogate illegal frontier crossers, held in camps while their fate was decided. At the end of the 1940s, hundreds of thousands of people were on the move, most trying to escape from countries under communist control. But, in February 1951, he was summoned by his commanding officer and shown two photographs.

> "If you see either of these men you will report that information to a senior officer immediately, do you hear?" If he could not find a senior officer, he was ordered to arrest the pair himself. Their names, he learned a few days later, courtesy of the *Daily Express*, were Guy Burgess and Donald Maclean, members of the British Foreign Service suspected of spying for the Soviet Union. (Sisman, 2015, p. 99)

As mentioned in Chapter 2, Cornwell was run by George Leggett, whom he admired, and was ready to do anything required of him—in one instance, becoming a temporary communist.

> David joined the Oxford University Communist Club, which met, supposedly in secret, on Sundays at Lyons' café in Cornmarket. At least one member noticed that David seemed unusually inquisitive about others present. According to another member of the Club, David was different: "he wasn't one of us." This same witness, speaking forty years afterwards, remembered him as "very withheld," with "a terrifying reticence." At a meeting of the local branch of the Anglo-Soviet Friendship Society, David met the Soviet Cultural Attaché, who was often in Oxford, bringing Russian vodka to woo undergraduates. Since he seemed interested, David was invited to an evening party at the Soviet Embassy in London. (…). At one stage in the courtship, the Cultural Attaché suggested that it might be "more fun" to meet outside the Embassy, and suggested a rendezvous between the two of them at a pub in Victoria. Then, without explanation, David was suddenly dropped, perhaps because the mask had slipped. (Sisman, 2015, p. 128)

Line management was not always successful: sometimes it was the runner's fault; at other times, the agent's. When in Graz, Cornwell had been recruited for a top-secret mission by an air intelligence officer (AIO) that required a trip to the Austrian/Yugoslav border to meet a high-ranking officer in the Czech Air Force who was allegedly willing to supply precious intelligence in exchange for cash. Concealed in his waistband, Cornwell had a heavy 9 mm Browning pistol. The meeting was to take place in a bar in a village on the Austrian side. The AIO entered first, followed by David, who was carrying a briefcase containing money. The AIO ordered two beers, and then pointed toward a billiards table, asking Cornwell if he fancied a game. Cornwell agreed, but "as he stooped to play the ball, he was startled by the clang of metal on the tiled floor; by the time he realised what had happened and bent to retrieve his weapon, the inn had emptied. 'Abort,' ordered the AIO, pausing only to finish his beer" (Sisman, 2015, p. 103).

Double agents (MI5)

Running double agents
According to his wife, double agent Eddie Chapman (Zigzag) did whatever M15 told him to do, but

> ... "[t]he moment Eddie did anything they didn't like, they thought something up about him," Betty Chapman says of his intelligence handlers. "They were really wicked to him. They never at any time recognised him as doing anything worthwhile." They spread the false rumour that he had slept with young girls to give them venereal diseases, and portrayed him as an unprincipled blackmailer. (Booth, 2007, loc. 211)

As for the Germans, they provided every agent with a "protector," usually a much older man, with the idea of creating a sort of paternal relationship. The protector saw to it that each agent had the correct papers, good food, and cigarettes, and often sat with the radio operator when the agent was sending his transmissions. Chapman's protector even visited him when he was feeling ill after reacting badly to some medicine (Booth, 2007).

Chapman's tasks for the Germans included sabotaging the De Havilland factory that manufactured Mosquito bombers, sending information regarding the inflow of US troops into Britain, and establishing the positions of antiaircraft defenses around London. He was assured that he would be well paid for such information, but, as MI5 predicted, the Germans lied to Chapman: "Breaking its promises was typical of how the

Abwehr treated its agents. They were usually paid late or sometimes not at all; requests for help were mysteriously never received; and more than a few were left hanging in the most dangerous circumstances imaginable" (Booth, 2007, loc. 3320)

MI5 gave agents their own "case officers," who were much more than administrative handlers: they took care of the agent's welfare, but also checked that messages sent to the Germans were properly formulated. As there was a rule that there should be no direct contact between SHAEF (Supreme Headquarters Allied Expeditionary Force) deception staff and the agents, it was the case officer who went to the office at Norfolk House to receive the information to be conveyed to the Germans through his agent, and then made sure that the message was transferred correctly (García and West, 2011, p. 200). The biographers of Harry Williamson (Tate) claimed that the case officer monitored his agent daily and kept track of previously reported activities.

> Those who controlled Tate as a double agent, Tar Robertson, William Luke, Russell Lee and the radio operator Ronnie Reed, of course, had regular briefings to discuss the agent Tate they had created, and to analyse his previous activities. All the time, the risk of disclosure to the German side was a dark cloud hanging over the business. They realised that they had built him into a first-class agent, but of "low grade"—that is, all the information originated from him, and it consisted almost entirely of material he himself had collected. (Jonason and Olsson, 2011, p. 61)

Obviously, both sides were somewhat suspicious of their double agents. MI5 kept all their agents apart in order to minimize leaks. The Abwehr put Williamson to the test:

> Tate was promised [by the Germans] that, at the end of April 1941, a man with £300 and a new crystal for his radio equipment would arrive. The man who was supposed to arrive was Karel Richter, who, however, had a much more sinister mission than to deliver money and a crystal—he was going to investigate whether Tate was a double agent. (Jonason and Olsson, 2011, p. 81)

Richter was captured two days after being parachuted into England. During interrogations, it was obvious that Richter was terrified: h e was convinced that a German invasion was underway and that the Gestapo would get hold of protocols made by the British. To be on the safe side, D.I. Wilson, one of Tate's case officers, conducted a fresh evaluation of Tate's work, showing convincingly that it was difficult, if not impossible, for the enemy to engage Tate in any disinformation projects.

Ultimately, the Germans became convinced of Tate's loyalty: "Karl Praetorius, one of the senior officers at the Abwehr in Hamburg, had said: 'Tate is our finest pearl. If he is a fake, then the whole necklace is false'" (Jonason and Olsson, 2011, p. 89). Further:

> When Tate sent his 1,000th message, announced on 21 September 1944, the Abwehr made exceptional efforts to establish his bona fides. A special committee was set up, with General Maurer as chairman, regarded as the most scrupulous and careful of judges, and composed of the most hard-boiled intelligence experts, communications experts, and even a psychiatrist. Their conclusion was that he had indeed transmitted valuable messages, and had done a good job. (Jonason and Olsson, 2011, p. 111)

As for Chapman, he was frequently scrutinized by his German handlers: "Despite the seeming trust they had placed in him, Eddie [Agent Zigzag] was constantly being questioned about his work in Britain. His various Abwehr cronies seemed to be working on the principle that a double agent would always remember the truth but never be able to repeat lies convincingly" (Booth, 2007, loc. 4153). Booth added, "The probing went on for days. This smiling controller with grey hair—who Eddie later learned was a psychologist—even got him drunk to test the reliability of his story" (2007, loc. 4160).

Spanish double agent Juan Pujol García (Garbo) enjoyed a high standing with the Germans, who groomed him to serve as an advanced observation post, guiding the V-1 flying bombs onto their targets (García and West, 2011). They asked him to record the times and positions of V-1 hits in London. The Germans responded to his signals and messages with detailed questionnaires, which provided MI5 with valuable intelligence, as they revealed weak areas in Germany's knowledge of Allied plans. Nevertheless, MI5 had a dilemma:

> If they, through their double agents, reported accurate information, it would be helpful for the Germans, while false information would threaten to expose double agents. (…) The solution to the dilemma was that agents' reports would exaggerate the number of rockets which hit London's northern and western parts, while the number of rockets which hit south and east London were minimised in the same manner. Based on these manipulated reports the Germans should conclude that the V1 rockets flew too far, and therefore reduce the range, which they did. (Jonason and Olsson, 2011, p. 131)

The Germans believed that García had a network, and from their perspective, it was very successful:

> There were no complaints, no recriminations for all the misinformation that had been conveyed over the previous two and a half years. Every plausible word of the deception campaign had been swallowed whole by the enemy. DAGOBERT's [García's German pseudonym] ring was held in such esteem that MI5 were determined to wring every last advantage from it. (García and West, 2011, p. 174)

Serbian triple agent Dušan Popov (Tricycle) traveled between London and Lisbon and made direct, face-to-face contact with the Abwehr, which rendered his situation more complex. All the information that Popov took with him to Lisbon had been vetted by MI5. It was usually a combination of correct, but harmless, information that was intended to raise his status as an agent in the eyes of the Abwehr and disinformation designed to deceive the German high command, but coherent with intelligence delivered by other double or triple agents. It was hoped that much of the verbal information Popov was expected to deliver would heighten German paranoia about an impending invasion.

At certain times, the Germans were disappointed with the information Popov delivered to them in Lisbon. It had to be addressed.

> Popov met with UK agent Ian Wilson in New York. Wilson's brief was to prepare the Yugoslav in every way possible to answer all the tricky questions he was likely to face when he arrived in Lisbon and was confronted by his controller, von Karsthoff, once again. Wilson handed over extensive notes setting out exactly what Popov needed for his cover story, including details of how he had supposedly obtained a radio set and operator, and a complete record of the intelligence that had been transmitted to Lisbon on his behalf. Wilson stressed that suitable sources would have to be attributed to everything and that they needed to be real people, preferably people whom Popov had met and could describe. (Miller, 2004, loc. 2743–2750)

Fortunately, when Popov returned to Lisbon, his controller did not ask any anxiety-inducing questions—possibly, von Karsthoff wanted to rehabilitate his agent to enhance his own reputation. In fact, it might be said that Popov's job in Lisbon was relatively straightforward:

> Popov was given instructions on how to contact British intelligence in Lisbon. He was to call Lisbon 52346 from a public telephone box and make an appointment for the following day, and then meet at the tennis pavilion at Tapada Ajuda an hour before the time stated. Alternatively, he could pass on

a message on the same telephone number. If he mentioned that it was a lovely day and he was enjoying the sunshine, it would mean that the Germans suspected nothing and everything was going well. If he said he thought a storm was brewing and it was likely to rain, it would mean that the Germans suspected something and he was not happy with his position. If he said the party was over, it would mean that he had been found out and that his position was "completely brûlé" (burned). (Miller, 2004, loc. 1727–1736)

It was in the relationships with, and between, his employers that things could become more complicated. First, there were tensions between MI5, responsible for counterespionage within the British Isles, and MI6, which collected intelligence overseas. As Lisbon was overseas, MI6 wanted Popov to extricate from von Karsthoff information about his personal enemies in Lisbon, about the Abwehr's relationship with the Gestapo, and about arrangements made for evacuation from Portugal if the war took a still more unfavorable turn for Germany. MI5 didn't like this extra task for their agent.

Second, despite London's assurances, the FBI was deeply suspicious about Popov and kept him under continuous surveillance: "He was surreptitiously followed everywhere by FBI agents whose orders were to check if he was being tailed by German agents" (Miller, 2004, loc. 1879–1886).

However, all these complications paled into insignificance when preparations for Operation Fortitude[4] began in February 1944:

Case officers had daily meetings at SHAEF (…) to concoct the information that would be fed to the enemy, like pieces of a jigsaw, to create a wholly false picture. The risks were horrendous. If one piece failed to fit, the whole charade could be exposed, leading to the danger that the Germans would start reading the agents' message "in reverse" and thereby accurately divine Allied intentions. The analogy drawn by MI5 was musical: the "orchestra" of double agents all needed to be playing the same symphony in tune. Those agents in whom the Germans reposed special trust were given the leading role in Operation Fortitude and were known as the "first violins." Tricycle, of course, was a "first violin." (Miller, 2004, loc. 4192–4199)

---

[4] The Second World War military deception deployed from March to June 1944 by the Allies in preparation for the Normandy landings.

Garbo was another "first violin" in Operation Fortitude, judging from his role in the invasion of Normandy:

> ... on the eve of the invasion of Normandy in June 1944. Juan Pujol García, a double agent operated by Britain under the code name Garbo, warned the Germans of the coming invasion just hours before it happened. As the invasion began to unfold exactly as he had warned, his credibility and importance rose in German estimation. Three days later, he sent another warning, saying that the Normandy attack was a diversion meant to draw forces away from the more massive, intended landing area in Pas de Calais. German intelligence believed Pujol, and the Germans continued to maintain the bulk of their ground forces in Pas de Calais through the end of June. When they realized they had been duped, it was too late. (Bar-Joseph, 2017, p. 50)

Impression management

Popov was judged by British intelligence to be an asset, as he was able to travel back and forth between London and Lisbon under the cover of being a lawyer negotiating import and export deals. MI5 relied a great deal on Popov's considerable talents as an actor and encouraged him to talk freely on all possible general topics like morale, food, or air raids in London, but he was also given specific information to pass on.

Network management

As mentioned in Chapter 3, García's network was partly invented. There was Agent No. 4, a subagent created thanks to García's friends in the hotel business, who supplied him with writing paper with the headings of leading West End hotels. This was camouflage for Garbo's secret letters sent by airmail. Another subagent, Agent 4(2), was supposed to be a guard at Chislehurst Caves in southeast London and a source of information for Agent No. 4 about activities within the caves. This explained why Agent No. 4 was not giving too much first-hand information, which might have been suspicious.

Williamson (Tate), on the other hand, was a loner and, with the approval of his runners, did not build a subagent network. Nevertheless, he played his part in Operation Fortitude, daily sending Germans false reports of troop concentration and information regarding fictitious battle orders.

As for enemy activities, according to Miller (2004), what the Abwehr believed to be their efficient espionage network in Britain was completely controlled by MI5. Some 120 German spies worked for the Allies during the Second World War; 39 of these were double agents. This was possible partly because the Abwehr, directed by Wilhelm Canaris, was badly organized and riddled with internecine rivalry. Abwehr case officers competed to raise their agents' reputation and through that their own status.

Informer management

Popov was aided by a particular piece of technology:

> [In New York], Popov received by letter eleven microdots which, when developed, contained a daunting list of extraordinarily complex and demanding questions about aircraft production, the development of rocket-aeroplanes, exports of iron and steel, armament production, the shipping of foodstuffs and raw materials and the disposition of army and naval units. Popov was told to try and recruit informers in various government offices. (Miller, 2004, loc. 2599–2606)

The Germans, on the other hand, prepared the following kind of questions for Popov to answer when he was in the United Kingdom:

> On one occasion, the questionnaire contained thirty-nine points, many concerning the prime minister: What are Churchill's prospects at the moment of remaining at the helm? How is his health? Is Churchill's loss of prestige through his last much criticised radio speech really so great that his position has been shaken? Does he by any chance already think of retiring and, if so, when? Who, with the present changed political situation in England, might be considered as his successor? (Miller, 2004, loc. 4431)

SOE

Running agents

Vera Atkins, the "spymistress," apparently took very good care of her agents:

> She had coaxed a sympathetic squadron leader to lend her an RAF rescue boat to plant Rolande Colas on her first mission. The girl had made her way from the coast to Paris to discuss the raising of resistance armies, and returned to rendezvous with the boat at a set time. The twelve-day operation netted hard and current facts that otherwise would have been difficult to glean. Vera later parachuted her back in, despite the objections raised by the chief of the air staff, Charles Portal, who thought there was "a vast difference in ethics" between dropping a spy from the air and "this entirely new scheme for dropping what one can only call assassins." (Stevenson, 2011, p. 142)

Colas became such a successful agent that she provoked suspicions about whether she had been turned by the enemy. At one point, Colas was forced to undergo a psychiatric check, after which she was told, "There's nothing wrong with you, except that nobody in their right mind would volunteer for your job" (Stevenson, 2011, p. 256). Atkins trusted Colas, and her concern for the agent was evident when she was sent on one of her missions to France:

> In a Moonlight Squadron hut, Rolande was searched by a man from Scotland Yard who then gave her a parachute, a Sorbo spine pad, a .38 Browning, a flick knife, and a wad of 50,000 French francs. All remaining English money, final personal effects, and a stray No. 25 bus ticket were stuffed into an envelope with her real name on it. Vera counted out some pills to the familiar litany. "This, if you've been a long time awake and need to keep going. This to knock out a German who pesters you. How you get it into him is up to you. These pills are for sleeping. And this one puts you to sleep for good." Then she shook her hand. Rolande thought for a moment that Vera really wanted to peck her on the cheek. (Stevenson, 2011, p. 258)

Such effective line management was not always appreciated by Atkins's bosses:

> ... Vera invited Zura [Jan Żurawski] to a weekend walking through the Sussex countryside around Winchelsea. There she outlined a mission involving dangers that even Zura had never faced. She needed a Polish-speaking pilot to fly solo in the Baltic area and record Russian wireless transmissions. These were not picked up in their entirety at Bletchley, and code breakers were not sure if transmissions originated in the Russian-occupied part of Poland. Zura flew a series of these spy missions, refueling at a secret base on the Finland–Sweden border. (...) He wrote me later: "The RAF's top brass resented Vera's 'irresponsible, unauthorized efforts to influence policy' and saw her as an interfering woman, uneducated in the traditions and disciplines of a fighting service." (Stevenson, 2011, p. 203)

Of course, agents could also make mistakes, and it was the runners' responsibility to deal with them. SOE officer and Second World War cryptographer Leo Marks tried to anticipate errors before they occurred:

> Leo Marks was always fearful of losing agents because their messages got unintentionally scrambled. He became alarmed whenever he caught someone like Violette Szabo repeatedly making mistakes that seemed so tiny but could endanger an entire network. He made new agents understand how they might accidentally produce these "indecipherables" while encoding under deadly pressure: cold, hungry, and lonely, trying to recall preselected words from

"recognition poems," injecting safety checks, tapping out Morse while enemy radio-locator vans searched for them. The Germans honed their detection skills to shut down power stations in sequence until a sudden suspension of dit-dit-dahs betrayed the agent's location. To counter this, batteries were used for a new batch of wireless sets, and crude ways were devised to crank them up. (Stevenson, 2011, p. 208)

Impression management

One of Atkins's agents, the Pole Krystyna Skarbek made six crossings from Hungary over the mountains to Poland, and another eight crossings through Slovak borders, but then her luck ran out. On January 24, 1941, the Hungarian police arrested her and delivered her to the Gestapo. There, she insisted that she was a journalist and denied having any British friends.

> She chewed her own tongue until blood spilled over her clothing when the Gestapo seemed ready to move from rough questioning to torture. Between bouts of coughing, she said she suffered from tuberculosis. A sympathetic Hungarian doctor confirmed this. She was released and, thumbing her nose at the Gestapo thugs who thought she had furtive reasons for knowing the British, went straight to the British legation. The minister, Sir Owen O'Malley, told her to get out of Hungary before worse things happened, and issued her a British passport in the name of Christina Granville. Then he hid her in the trunk of his official car and drove her over the border into Yugoslavia. In Belgrade, she delivered to the British legation the last of the microfilm she regularly collected from Poland, hidden in her ski gloves. (Stevenson, 2011, p. 163)

According to Stevenson (ibid.), O'Malley said later that Skarbek was the bravest person he had ever met.

Stockholm, Defense Staff

Running agents

During the Second World War, Stockholm was described as a "Casablanca of the North": allegedly, it was teeming with agents, double agents, and spy catchers from many different countries (Agrell, 2006, 2017). The Swedes collected intelligence under the auspices of both the Swedish Armed Forces (Defense Staff) and the Swedish Police, which were seldom in conflict with each other. Agents for the Defense Staff were numerous and varied:

> One agent for the Staff appeared to be high up in Stockholm Nazi circles; several others reported from communist circles, of which at least one seems to have been employed at the Headquarters of the Communist Party. Many of the agents seemed to have had their daily work assigned to various central authorities, companies and interest groups. There were also several cafes, hotels and other meeting places in Stockholm, where foreigners, refugees and others used to gather, and from which the Staff regularly received information. (Thunberg, 2009, p. 175)

Spies from alien countries were identified by mapping their networks and gathering trivial details, combined with scouting and monitoring. This way of working in counterespionage had been learned by intelligence staff at courses run by the Abwehr in Berlin.

The Defense Staff had a unit called C-bureau, which recruited many women as couriers, infiltrators, informants, or escorts. It was taken for granted that they would offer sex. C-bureau paid for abortions and wrote "dentist" on the invoices. Indeed, it was actually a dentist who performed the abortions with dentistry equipment, with varying results (Bergman, 2014).

As mentioned in Chapter 2, one of the best-known women agents was Karin Lannby, who, in 1940–1941, was in a relationship with Ingmar Bergman. She mostly received her instructions at particular locations in the city, which had coded names and were often changed. Sometimes messages were left for her at a hotel reception. She also received some instruction by post. This was originally via an address of her colleague, who, at one point, reported her to the police as a possible Soviet agent. The police constantly monitored Lannby, as she was suspected to be both a German and a Soviet spy, until the Defense Staff finally informed them that Lannby was their agent.

In 1942, encouraged by the Defense Staff, Lannby contacted Kulturabteilung, a department at the German Embassy, and secured a part-time job as a secretary of the German journalist Winfried Martini. She wrote so many reports—some 1300 concerning around 17000 people—that the police, who were responsible for archiving, decided to abandon their strict dating of the reports.

In November 1943, Lannby received a new task from the Defense Staff—an infiltration—to which she gladly agreed. It concerned the new Swedish South European Information Office, a private enterprise run by a German businessman, Karl Christian von Loesch, who, with the help of the Hungarian state, was supposed to clean up Hungary's negative reputation and advertise the country's newly democratic approach.

Lannby became employed as a secretary and did most of her work in the office, without a salary. In a tough economic climate, Lannby threatened the Swedish South European Information Office with court and an accusation of breach of contract. She was then subjected to mafia-style threats by three men from the Hungarian Mission (Bergman, 2014, p. 244). She asked the police for protection, or at least a weapon, but got nothing:

> By police she was from the start seen as a competitor. She belonged to a category that officially did not exist. She was not employed; she could not turn to any union or occupational group. She simply did not exist in the male hierarchy of the country's defenders. It was a painful discovery. (Thunberg, 2009, p. 345)

Even the Defense Staff did not support her. They "exiled" her to Gothenburg (from where she was recalled in August 1944, when another agent fell ill). In exile, she wrote a mocking letter to three department heads at the Security Police. She accused them of constant persecution and refusing to protect her. She revealed some embarrassing errors in their activity and signed the letter with the names of the bosses of three principal foreign spy organizations in Sweden—German, English, and Soviet—showing how much inside knowledge she had (Bergman, 2014).

Women agents struggled to earn respect. In C-bureau, they were called "sirens," from a Swedish slang expression "street sirens," that is, prostitutes. Here is an interview with one of the officials from C-bureau:

> — Are they "sirens" in the familiar sense of the word?
> — Well, one can say that, to a certain degree, or some of them, at any rate. Most of them are from the countryside, easy to influence, easy to steer, not especially intelligent. They do what they're told to do. Some of them are classic informers, girls that in one way or another got the job at some foreign missions, organizations or companies that represent foreign interests, have some cover activities and such. (Bergman, 2014, p. 200)

Asked who was running the "sirens," and how, the interviewee answered that originally it was the C-bureau boss, but soon it was too much, even for him:

> This is why he tries to place them under other "runners," but it is difficult within the staff to find people who know how to run informers. Not many have [his] talents. He is incredible when dealing with women! Sometimes he swears at those "stupid girls" that demand so much of him, who lie so much, who try to flatter him so much, who take so much time. As if that weren't enough, they all insist on falling in love with him, these silly geese... Just how stupid can one be? Hard to believe that a man of his status and background should fall for one of those unintelligent country wenches? (Bergman, 2014, pp. 200–201)

The interviewer ended with a general commentary about the role of women in secret service work:

> Yes, one has to admit that they must have some primitive intelligence— otherwise they would be completely useless, but it is more a kind of cunning, female intelligence good for intrigues ... perhaps talent, as the word "intelligence" does not fit these women. They have a cunning talent, an inherited female instinct, which makes them fitting for this work ... and also these exemplars have those deliriously beautiful bodies, decisively an asset in this work. (Bergman, 2014, p. 201)

Impression management

Via one of her informants, Lannby got in touch with the German–Baltic Baron Boris Stackelberg, who had come to Sweden from Finland in 1940. He recruited her to inform the Germans about the dealings of Japanese diplomats in Sweden, as she had many contacts with various diplomats through encounters in nightclubs. She failed in this task, but collected enough information on Stackelberg, who was expelled from Sweden. Lannby was arrested to conceal the nature of her role. During an interrogation, Stackelberg said of her: "'She is an actress. And she liked to imagine being a Mata Hari. It was just a play that we both played. All this was simply invented so that her life should be more interesting'" (Thunberg, 2009, p. 233).

Network management

Women agents who worked for C-bureau created a network known as the "secretaries' club," which met weekly. They were encouraged by Lannby, who perceived the benefits of the spies sharing their experiences.

One of them had been arrested as a girlfriend of an unmasked German spy; another barely survived the "dentist's" intervention. The following exchange between "Inez" and "Gurli" reveals that several women spies had doubts about whether their work was worth it:

> … I don't know if I want to continue with this. I do not think, like you [Gurli], that it is so fantastic that we are paid. I became disgusted with all this. Ok, I do like to eat well, drink well, dance … after all, we go to the best places. They buy us clothes and jewelry, but we must pay for it, actually. It is not free of charge, and you know it…
>
> — A bit of sex, what's wrong with that? If you know what to do, it will go quickly. They are always drunk, after all. I don't care; I only don't want to be pregnant again.
>
> —I begin to think that it is tough. (…) Sweaty, stinky Germans who cling on you, and who want "to know each other," and put their dirty fingers everywhere, with bad breath. Yak! It is not worth it, Gurli. And then you have to sit down and write about it, and go through it once more—for God knows who reads the reports, and then be paid for what you have written. No, we are not better than those hookers on the street! (Bergman, 2014, pp. 128–129)

Indeed, according to Bergman, when four women took part in a sadistic orgy arranged for German officers, one almost died; she was taken to a mental hospital when she threatened to tell her story. This was "collateral damage," according to Ternberg, their boss in C-bureau.

Informer management
At the beginning of her service in 1939, Karin Lannby was told to focus on an Italian correspondent, Mario Vanni, who behaved strangely in public places and sent peculiar news and telegrams—the suspicion was that they were coded. Lannby went to tea dances at the same place as Vanni and was asked by him to dance, but only rarely. It didn't work—she wasn't to his taste, she reported.

She then transferred her attention to Ove Adlers, employed by the Swedish Confederation of Transport Enterprises, who was often seen in the company of a daughter of Clarence von Rosen, a well-known Swedish Nazi. Lannby learned that in Germany, Adlers had worked for a time at Hapag (Hamburg-Amerikanische Packertahrt-Aktien-Gesellschaft, known in English as the Hamburg America Line, a transatlantic shipping enterprise), famous for employing spies. She went to Fågel Blå, Adlers's favorite restaurant and used her theatrical talents to approach Adlers. She let him know that she was bored and was awaiting some fascinating job. She also admitted her previous interest in communism and how disappointed she was with it now. Adlers referred to Swedes as people with no discipline and no chance to achieve greatness; he also told her about his work for Hapag and prepared her for Stackelberg's arrival.

Other women at C-bureau also had different kinds of information-gathering jobs. The following scene is worth quoting in full:

> Two of Ternberg's [C-Bureau boss] girls took on a Belgian director, obviously a Jew, suspected of previously working for Comintern, and of contacts with NKVD/GPU. The Bureau put a lot of alcohol and cigarettes in a hotel room at Norra Smedjegatan, and a stenographer in the adjoining room. There was a hole in the wall behind a picture, and the stenographer was equipped with a device like a stethoscope, with cables ending with Bakelite props to put in the ears. He was to note down phonetically all that he heard.
>
> The evening started well. The Belgian, calling himself Monsieur Cheval, by others called Stallion, as he constantly talked about his conquests, was invited into a horse cab at Strand Hotel. He had already had a great many alcoholic beverages. But when he was forced to go up the narrow stairs at the Norra Smedjegatan hotel, he became suspicious and unhappy. Gurli and Emily decided to use all their charms to get him in a better mood. They undressed almost totally, only keeping on their sophisticated underwear, lit him a cigar and plied him with alcohol.
>
> The man spoke very poor Swedish, and many misunderstandings happened. The two girls didn't understand the man's peculiar French. Ternberg's collaborators in the next room thought the guy could be Flemish—but why did he have a French surname?
>
> Soon the man gave up French and started speaking much better German, so that the girls began to think that he was a German agent. But when Stallion wanted to begin "more bodily activities," particular body parts refused to play ball, and he started swearing in Russian. When his long and partly incomprehensible tirades were translated afterwards, at least one sentence became completely clear: "Here I got the attention of the youngest and most attractive Swedish swallows, and the bloody bulb will not get up!" (Bergman, 2014: p. 149)

The information collected was limited to the revelation that Soviet agents used the term "swallows" to describe female Swedish agents. C-bureau didn't learn anything about his spy activities, although they were able to establish that he was a German–Jewish communist working for the Soviets. They stopped calling him Stallion and called him Bulb instead.

1955–1975

United Kingdom, MI5 and MI6

Running agents

In his biography of Cornwell, Sisman (2015) described in some detail one of the intelligence officers whom Cornwall knew well, John Bingham, 7th Baron Clanmorris. According to Sisman, Bingham did not want to be promoted, as the role of agent runner suited him well.

One of Bingham's agents worked under very stressful conditions and had to be debriefed every evening. Another infiltrated the Communist Party as a typist in the early 1950s and had worked her way up to the position of personal assistant to its General Secretary. She regularly provided reports and copies of documents to MI5, giving them to Bingham during cricket matches. Cornwell, who often acted as Bingham's deputy, believed that Bingham was loved by his agents and that they worked for him rather than for their country.

Cornwell and Bingham often worked in tandem:

> At eleven o'clock one morning David was warned that an important woman agent he was running was in peril: a telephone tap had revealed that she had been blown. (…). David consulted Bingham, and within an hour they had devised a plan to suggest that she had been supplying information to a newspaper rather than to MI5. In the guise of an investigative journalist, David wrote a string of letters to his agent, thanking her for the information received so far and imploring her to reveal more details of her work. He and Bingham then had the forgery section provide stamped and postmarked envelopes, extending back in time over a period of weeks. They fed the letters into the envelopes, sealed them and slit them open again. (…) Meanwhile David had sent a covert message to his agent, instructing her to tell her employers that she had toothache needing urgent treatment. At "the dentist" she was handed the letters to place in her handbag and told to leave it on her desk when she next left the office, in the knowledge that it would be searched while she was out. Telephone checks confirmed that her employers had taken the bait. Though she was compromised the immediate danger had been averted, and she was gradually withdrawn. (Sisman, 2015, p. 203)

In his own memoir, Cornwell remembered "Harry," a double agent who he had run many years before:

> With our help he had schooled himself to think and react from the hip as one of [Party's] faithful. Yet he always managed to come up smiling for his weekly debriefings with his case officer: All right then, Harry? I would ask.

"Hunky-dory, thanks. How's your good self and the missus?" Harry had taken on all the Party's dirty jobs, in the evenings and on weekends, that other comrades were only too glad to be relieved of. He had sold or failed to sell the *Daily Worker* at street corners, ditched his unsold copies and turned in the cash we gave him to cover them. He had acted as runner and talent-spotter for visiting Soviet cultural attachés and third secretaries of the KGB, and accepted their dreary assignments to collect tittle-tattle about technical industries in the area where he lived. And if no tittle-tattle came his way, we provided him with that too, having first made sure it was harmless. (le Carré, 2016, p. 200)

In fact, "Harry" never brought in any useful information. To comfort him, his runner repeatedly told him that, if the Soviets attacked Britain, he would end up in an important position, from which he would be able to run an effective resistance movement. Cornwell had the feeling that Harry believed this as little as he did, but it helped to raise Harry's morale.

Impression management
In the 1960s, Cornwell moved (or was moved) to MI6. His first posting was Bonn, and he was the British Embassy's Second Secretary, with the task of traveling around Germany. His overt role required him to cultivate German politicians and journalists—a difficult task since he was disgusted by the presence of former Nazis:

> His task was to investigate and detect potential Nazi cells or organisations, and to recruit German sleepers who would join any such groupings in order to provide information on them. But since the Germans were extremely sensitive about the possibility of any British interference in their politics, David's function had to be concealed from all but a very few senior members of the Embassy staff. (…). Nor did he have much to do with the [MI6] station itself, because his work was peripheral to its main effort against the Eastern bloc countries, the Soviet Union in particular. He never had anything to do with running agents into East Germany, for example. His remit left him his own master, on his own for much of the time. As it turned out, there was very little for him to do, because the feared Nazi revival never materialized. (Sisman, 2015, p. 218)

Israel, Mossad

Running agents
The cases of two Egyptians who worked for Mossad illustrate the very different ways in which running an agent can end. In the first case, the

difficulties concerned the agent; the second could be called a case of mismanagement.

The Egyptian spy Ashraf Marwan was known as "the Angel," but, as Bar-Joseph pointed out, running him was not a simple task:

> For starters, he didn't take the basic steps needed to ensure his security. Despite being given alternative phone numbers, for the first few months he kept calling up the Israeli embassy in London to set up meetings. To get him to stop, Dubi [one of his runners] set up an offsite phone line manned by a go-between known as a "dead letter box." Marwan was told to call that number, rather than the embassy (…) The go-between was a London woman in her fifties who rarely left home. Whenever Marwan called, she immediately contacted Dubi. At just around this time, the first answering machines had been introduced, and Dubi installed one in the apartment so that Marwan could call at any time of night.
>
> Yet Marwan continued to take needless risks. At least once he arrived at a meeting in an Egyptian embassy car, with an Egyptian embassy driver. Another time, Dubi and Meir Meir [another runner] met Marwan in his apartment in London's Mayfair district. The entire time they were talking in the living room, a local prostitute was waiting for Marwan in the bedroom. (…) Marwan didn't care.
>
> He took risks in the documents he brought, as well. Many of them were originals—not even photocopies. When Dubi asked why he wasn't worried about getting caught with the documents, he just smiled and said, "They won't search me." (2017, p. 125)

Marwan would meet with Dubi when he traveled to Europe—as part of an official delegation, on business, or on holidays. After the first few meetings he began receiving US$10,000 per set of meetings; later, he asked to double the fee. Seeing the doubts, he threatened to cut off contact, and they paid as requested.

Not that this ended the problems. A few months after Marwan started working with Mossad in 1971, at their meeting in London, Dubi noticed a handgun sticking out from behind Marwan's jacket. When asked, Marwan drew it out and offered it to Dubi; aghast, Dubi told Marwan that in London even mafia bosses didn't carry firearms. Marwan explained that he had a diplomatic passport, and the local authorities couldn't do anything to him. Marwan brought another gun to the next meeting, nicely packed. Dubi took the gun and thanked Marwan.

Another Mossad agent, Eli Cohen was sent to Buenos Aires in 1961 to establish his cover as a Syrian émigré (Hamidi, 2019). In February 1962, he moved to Damascus. During his last visit to Israel, in November 1964, Eli told his runners that he was afraid and wished to terminate his assignment in Syria. When Mossad asked him to return to Syria one more time, he agreed, but became far less careful in his transmissions, sometimes calling once or even twice a day, almost always at the same time. It was later interpreted by some as an expression of cockiness, by others as a suicidal wish:

> If Cohen and his Israeli controllers had only been more cautious, his chances of survival would have been higher. (…) Unfortunately, Cohen's case officers did not pay attention to the warning signs. They were too focused on preparing for conflict, because there was another bout of tension on the border. (…) In 2015, then-Mossad head Tamir Pardo told Nadia [Cohen's wife] that it was wrong to send Eli back to continue his mission in Syria. Upon returning to Damascus, Cohen forgot the rules of prudence. His broadcasts became more frequent, and in the space of five weeks he sent 31 radio transmissions. His case officers in Tel Aviv should have restrained him, but none did. The material he was sending was just too good to stop. (Melman, 2019)

Impression management

This was less of a concern for Marwan (he didn't even make an effort), than for his handler. Dubi had joined Mossad only in 1968, yet his superior officer gave him the role of Marwan's runner—despite the fact that, at the start of Marwan's service, top officers had specified that he should be run by an experienced intelligence officer. Dubi managed to create the impression that his first loyalty was to Marwan rather than Mossad, that he could defend Marwan's interests against his superiors.

The higher-ups were not happy. They suspected Dubi of "defecting" to Marwan's side—intelligence agencies take steps to avoid an overly close connection between a single handler and an agent over a long period of time, for practical (What if the handler becomes ill?) and security reasons. Handlers will be changed from time to time, or a second handler will be added. However, Marwan rejected any suggestion of replacing Dubi, and if the issue was mentioned, he threatened to quit. The solution was somewhat unusual: Dubi was replaced by his boss, Zvi Zamir, "a former general in the legendary Israeli army, who now headed the most storied intelligence agency on earth" (Bar-Joseph, 2017, p. 127). After all, they knew from the beginning that behind Marwan's decision to work for Mossad were psychological needs for recognition.

As for Cohen, soon after he arrived in Buenos Aires in February 1961, he successfully integrated himself into the social and cultural life of the Syrian community. In Buenos Aires, he was known as a wealthy businessman who was generous, tipped well, and loved the night life.

The story went that he had 17 lovers in Syria, all beauties belonging to powerful families. Apparently, both Cohen and Mossad hoped that these women would help him escape in case of a crisis. They didn't.

When Cohen moved to Damascus in 1962, he carried with him a powerful miniature radio transmitter hidden in the false bottom of a food mixer (the cord of his electric razor serving as the antenna), cyanide tablets disguised as aspirin, high-explosive chemicals hidden in toothpaste tubes and cans of shaving cream, and the finest camera equipment. He rented an apartment across the street from the Syrian Army Headquarters, in which he set up an import–export business. His shipped furniture had hollowed legs where he could hide microfilms and notes, which went to Israel via Zurich.

Cohen was eventually discovered by Syrian counterintelligence and executed in 1965.

1977–1989

Poland, Ministry of Interior Affairs (MIA), Departments I, II

Running agents
Filip Hagenbeck—"an ordinary spy," as he called himself—began his career by both collecting and analyzing information provided by the Third World Team. When his superior officer had reservations about something in the analysis, a process called "sculpting" began: the intelligence officer first defended his theses and observations before the team leader, and then they both went to the boss. If their arguments were not accepted, the second round began. Finally, the intelligence thus analyzed became the "intelligence information," which was passed on.

After a year, Hagenbeck was promoted to inspector and transferred to the Ideological Diversion Team. One of his tasks was to convince General Jaruzelski (then the Communist Party's First Secretary and leader of Poland) to allow an exchange of six CIA spies for one Polish. The letter he was to write had to be "seductive," he was told by his bosses:

> ... in intelligence work, writing is a utilitarian art. It must meet numerous conditions, including one of the most important—defined by the neat KISS acronym. Americans developed it as Keep It Short (and) Simple. (...). Why? Because our recipients are usually overwhelmed with dozens of documents. And they don't have time to study them. (Hagenbeck, 2019, pp. 280–281, transl. BC)

In 1985, Hagenbeck was finally transferred to operations in Department II, which was responsible for counterintelligence. His targets were the FBI and the Defense Intelligence Agency. Finally, he was sent abroad to Nigeria, where he could start building his own network. In contrast to British intelligence, the MIA assumed it to be far more preferable if the officer who recruited the agent was not his or her runner, unless there were no other options, to avoid an overly close relationship.

Intelligence gathering could be a delicate operation—as illustrated by a journalist's question for agent Vincent Severski:

> I: Is it necessary to go to bed with someone for work?
> S: Personally, I have not been in this situation. I have never issued such a work order. But adults work in our organization. There is no intelligence worker who would not consider such a thing. Although in my time it did not happen to officers. But when it comes to sources—yes. I had a woman agent who could get incredible info this way. But I warn against judging this by traditional criteria. Anyway, special services have worse things on their conscience than just morally or ethically dubious acts. (...) I would say that when it comes to the moral side of work, activities in the intimate sphere are not the most dramatic. (...) After all, every intelligence organization is a criminal organization. We serve to break the laws of other countries. Our task is to get information that the opponents do not want to give us, so they wrap it with security clauses. For us, information not covered by any security classification is actually not worth anything... [5]

Impression management

As mentioned earlier, Hagenbeck's first job at the MIA was collecting and analyzing information for the Third World Team, within his specialist area—Jewish organizations active in English-speaking countries. He was also required to evaluate the informational and operational work of officers serving abroad (each of them came back for a vacation after two years). However, his legend made him an employee of the Territorial Defense Inspectorate (a part of the Polish Armed Forces), working to mitigate the effects of nuclear attacks, but located in MIA's neighborhood.

Network management

In the 1980s, when MIA's Department II sent Hagenbeck to Nigeria, his task there was to find informants, with the potential for the office to

---

[5]   https://www.polityka.pl/tygodnikpolityka/kraj/1517024,1,rozmowa-z
-bylym-agentem-polskiego-wywiadu.read, accessed June 28, 2011, transl. BC.

register particular people as agents; such registration opened access to information about that person:

> ... it could turn out that this diplomat (...) or just a guest from Nigerian television—is already being worked out by, for example, the Bulgarians, and I should stay away from him or send everything I get to the Office. In this way we could offer the Bulgarians what I have obtained, and in return get something that interests us especially and which we currently do not have access to. (...) And so by buddying—today we would say "networking"—the folders multiplied. And tasks related to them. (Hagenbeck, 2019, p. 415, transl. BC)

Successful registration enabled an agent to be paid and to be reimbursed for lunch and travel expenses. Keeping in touch with a local agent was not always easy, even under the cover of a diplomat:

> A foreign spy driving a car on diplomatic numbers is one such situation. Losing the observers was not complicated in the chaotic traffic on the roads of Nigeria. But what's next? Travelling on foot, as we practiced in Kiejkuty,[6] meant that every loyal snitch could notice my presence, especially in a place where the very presence of an *oyibo* [European] might have been surprising. And where it wasn't surprising, we expected cameras or the watchful eyes of people cooperating with counter-intelligence. One must remember that any undemocratic, authoritarian authority is afraid of opposition, coup and conspiracy. And foreign governments can support, finance, inspire such conspiracies.
>
> Intelligence has its own ways to deal with such threats. Personal meetings in such conditions are suspended. One will meet with the agent in another country. One will visit him in a hotel where he stopped on his way to a business meeting somewhere in Europe or anywhere else. (Hagenbeck, 2019, p. 508, transl. BC)

In Hagenbeck's opinion, attempts to recruit agents are always hampered by uncertainty. The intelligence officer must assess the costs of an unsuccessful recruitment and find ways to minimize them. The highest level of risk comes with attempts to recruit an alien intelligence officer within his own territory. If it works, the potential for success is enormous; if it fails, the recruiter can be arrested, even if protected by diplomatic immunity, and expelled from the country (if he is lucky).

---

[6]   Poland's main spy training center; see Chapter 5.

Informer management

When in Poland, Hagenbeck was required to maintain "an operational contact" with Polish citizens who were to visit the United States:

> You're going to California. West Coast. Do you know the concept of "Silicon Valley?" Yes, yes, I know that you are not an electronics engineer but a political scientist. That is why the FBI will sniff around you very carefully. We do not expect you to repeat the path of the Director of Pewex.[7] God forbid! But if the FBI—underlining the word "if"—starts taking an interest in you, then we want you to know what you can and cannot do. We can train you in this area so that you have at least a fair chance. We are very interested in how the FBI will play it. We have recognized over a dozen of their model behaviors, and we can share this knowledge with you. Because of course, once this happens, you can agree to all their proposals. And let them recruit you. But you probably like to sleep peacefully? (Hagenbeck, 2019, p. 316, transl. BC)

A common answer was, "Then I am not going!" Yet, if all went well, after a few days Hagenbeck would receive a call, the candidate telling him that, after having thought it over, he agreed to have "contact with [the Department] in terms of counter-intelligence protection against the aggressive activities of the US special services" (2019, pp. 317–318).

Then there was the requirement to learn the "intelligence situation in the area". For example, Hagenbeck had never been to Chicago, but he knew all the streets and the map of the subway, as well as the location of Polish stores, and of the FBI. As for the qualities of particular candidates, Hagenbeck said the following:

> Intelligence capabilities cannot be estimated and evaluated in a vacuum. The basis is the strategic or tactical interests of the state or service as a whole. The potential candidate for recruitment will be sussed out not because he or she exists and because I have access to him or her. It is not enough.
>
> A candidate must be useful in some sense for the intelligence—for example, as an independent carrier of important secrets desirable by our state, or as a potential intermediary in reaching real carriers. The history of world intelligence is full of stories of recruiting wives to make them uncover the secrets of their husbands. (2019, p. 502, transl. BC)

---

[7]   A Polish intelligence officer, Marian Zacharski, who was caught by the FBI, returned to Poland in a spy exchange and became director of Pewex, the state-owned company that sold imported items for foreign currency. In 1996, he was accused of mismanagement, https://pl.wikipedia.org/wiki/Marian _Zacharski, accessed August 18, 2022.

And here Hagenbeck is explaining the difference between agents and informants:

> An information contact (…) was valuable to us because he or she had valuable information or could explain the context or sense of what we already knew. Often, in-depth study proved that recruiting such a person for various reasons was not possible or advisable. But if such a person talks to me and reveals something, what is the need to recruit him or her?
>
> Such an IC often did not know or pretended he did not know that he was talking to a foreign intelligence representative. If the local counterintelligence caught him, he could always explain that he plays bridge with me and simply likes me. So the IC was not an agent. He was ... an information contact. (Hagenbeck, 2019, pp. 517–518, transl. BC)

AGENTS RUNNING IN THE FIELD[8]

There were many similarities among secret services in different countries in their approaches to the line management of agents, and the handling of informers by agents—partly due to the similar requirements of their jobs and partly because intelligence agencies imitated one another. In all intelligence agencies, there were internal conflicts and tensions, not to mention political pressures, but distinctive styles of line management did emerge in different countries.

The "British Style"

It could be summarized as "caretaking"—up to a point. Descriptions of the relationships between runners and agents were found to be very similar across British secret service organizations, especially in the case of double agents:

> Every double agent was lodged separately in a safe house and assigned an MI5 case officer, usually an older man, who was obliged to play many roles—part guardian, part companion, part social worker and, ultimately, jailer. Case officers were encouraged to develop close relationships with their charges, both to obviate any lingering feelings of guilt and to make the agent dependent on the case officer's goodwill. Providing the agent continued to cooperate, the case officer did everything in his power to ensure that his charge was comfortable and content, providing money, cigarettes, booze and, occasionally, discreet female company. (Miller, 2004, loc. 976)

---

[8]   John le Carré, *Agent Running in the Field* (2019).

These "close relationships" were not to be mistaken for friendship:

> There was little room for sentiment or friendship in the espionage business, as Wren and Wilson [Dušan Popov's runners] well knew. Calculations were made coldly and if one agent had to be sacrificed to protect others, then the sacrifice was made. It was the dark side of the great game. Both Wren and Wilson liked Popov enormously, and thought he was great fun and good company, as well as being a first-class agent. But their affection for him was not allowed to taint their judgement, and it did not. (Miller, 2004, loc. 2995–3003)

The "Soviet Style"

It could be best described as erratic, as it was mostly dictated by political events. This was especially visible in Stalin's time (until 1954), when intelligence officers could from one day to the next become "the enemies of the Party," as euphemistically termed by the official media. This meant that the fate of their agents was difficult to predict: the Soviets saved and celebrated three of the Cambridge Five, while Sorge waited in vain to be rescued from a Japanese prison.

The management of agents became less haphazard in the post-Stalin era, although it was far less efficient than the British approach. As for Poland, which until 1989 followed Soviet rules, Severski observed, "The work in Polish intelligence was often a wild ride, not like in MI5 or the CIA, where officers have health and safety rules."[9]

The "Israeli Style"

From the material collected here one might say that the Mossad style of line management was an amalgamation of British and Soviet methods. While Marwan was certainly treated "in a British way" (although it is doubtful that MI5 or MI6 would tolerate this type of eccentric behavior on the part of an agent), Cohen did not have such luck.

---

[9]   https://wyborcza.pl/magazyn/7,124059,20906654,vincent-v-severski -czekista-to-brzmi-dumnie-rozmowa.html, accessed October 28, 2016, transl. BC.

The "German Style"

The Germans adopted a style of management similar to the British in the initial stages (controller as "protector"), but changed tack later—breaking promises, ignoring requests for help, and not paying agents. The Abwehr certainly suffered from defective organization—whether its head Wilhelm Canaris mismanaged it on purpose, as part of his known attempts to get rid of Hitler,[10] it is difficult to say, but he was certainly sending classified information to the British. Nevertheless, Swedish intelligence officers took courses run by the Abwehr in Berlin, and followed their example.

The "Women's Style"

As for women managers, our source material included only two—Vera Atkins and Stella Rimington—who both fulfilled all the requirements of the British style. They treated their agents with care and respect, as long as the agents deserved it; this was appreciated by the agents, not so much by the higher-ups. Female agents were subjected to discrimination and paternalism, no matter which country. We intend to continue our research, analyzing the fate of women spies in greater detail.

---

[10] See, e.g., Bassett (2011).

7. Rewards and sanctions

The effective distribution of rewards is said to have a significant impact on the performance of employees. Attractive rewards enable organizations to recruit and retain high-quality people who contribute to the success of the organization. Reward management in standard organizations includes the design and implementation of systems that cover grade and pay structures, recognizing achievement and providing employee benefits. But money isn't everything, and Human Resource Management textbooks emphasize the role of nonfinancial rewards such as recognition, autonomy, learning and development opportunities, career progression, and increased responsibility.

REWARDS: INNOVATIVE WAYS OF PAYING

Secret service organizations are not known to be high payers, as illustrated by Stella Rimington's description of the MI5 approach:

> The motivation for people to work in this way is not money. Unlike major companies in the commercial sector, MI5 does not set out to offer top quartile executive pay with bonuses and share options. Motivation is complex. It comes from a combination of the intrinsic interest and excitement of the work itself (whether it is a painstaking espionage investigation or a fast-moving counter-terrorist operation) and a sense of the importance of the job to be done. There is also a strong sense of loyalty to the organisation, to colleagues and to the country, however that is defined and however unfashionable that may sound. It is a delicate balance to create and maintain. (2001, p. 179)

Money is the reward for service, but it is also used to pay off employees when they are no longer of use to the organization. Just as in standard organizations, some intelligence officers were reported to have been paid to leave to avoid scandal, as was the case with Kim Philby:

> C summoned his former protégé. Philby knew what was coming. According to some accounts, he may have offered to quit: "I'm no good to you now . . . I think you'd better let me go." In Philby's version of events, C told him, with "obvious distress," that he would have to ask for his resignation. His friend-

ship with Burgess, a Soviet spy, had rendered him useless for further work as an MI6 officer. The mere size of his payoff—£4,000, equivalent to more than £32,000 today—was proof that he was leaving with honour, and the support of his service. Philby could "not possibly be a traitor," Menzies told White. Philby pretended to be sanguine, accepting his role as a scapegoat. But Elliott was furious, and did nothing to hide his belief that a "dedicated, loyal officer had been treated abominably on the basis of evidence that was no more than paranoid conspiracy theory." (Macintyre, 2014, p. 164)

An additional perk of the job in MI5 and MI6 was exemption from paying taxes. Take, for example, Philby and his fellow intelligence officer Nicholas Elliott:

> Nicholas Elliott, meanwhile, was making a parallel career move. In the summer of 1941, he was also transferred to Section V, with responsibility for the Netherlands. Henceforth Philby would be fighting German espionage in the Iberian Peninsula, and Elliott would be doing the same in Nazi-occupied Holland, from the next-door office. Each would be paid a salary, in cash, of £600 a year and neither, in accordance with longstanding secret services rules, would pay any tax. (Macintyre, 2014, p. 27)

As the name suggests, double agents were paid double, making their position more lucrative than that of regular spies. For Juan Pujol García (Garbo), there was the added satisfaction of receiving plaudits and cash from those on the wrong end of his deception: "The Abwehr and the Wehrmacht high command seemed oblivious to the huge scale of the deception [by Garbo and his network], and perhaps the ultimate irony lay in the fact that GARBO was receiving constant praise and funds from the victims of his imaginative duplicity" (García and West, 2011, p. 174).

The risk for the actual employer was that the nominal employer would be more generous, and the spy might change his or her allegiances—the classic tension between external competitiveness ("the market pay") and the internal equity. Eddie Chapman (Zigzag) was a spy who benefited from his actual employer—the British—trying to match his German pay. He received generous remuneration from the Abwehr (his nominal employer), and his contract included reimbursement of "incidental expenses" and compensation for any period of imprisonment:

> One gloriously sunny morning that August, Eddie and the Baron [Baron Rittmeister Stefan von Gröning, Chapman's German controller] were sitting in the château's grounds together when Abwehr officer von Gröning removed a bulky envelope from his pocket. It contained a contract, written in English, between Fritz Graumann (Chapman's code name) and the Third Reich. Eddie

read the details and was delighted to see that he would receive 100,000 Reichsmarks—or, if he preferred it, the same amount in pounds sterling, at a rate of ten pounds to the mark—for his work. The contract was generous. While absent from France, a salary of 300 Reichsmarks a month would be paid into his account: if, for any reason, he was jailed in Britain, his fee would automatically go up to 600 Reichsmarks. He would be given £1,000 upon departure and all other incidental expenses would be reimbursed. (Booth, 2007, loc. 2056–2063)

MI5, Chapman's actual employer, worked on the principle of a "financial inducement" and a "war bond":

In early 1943, MI5 realised that a small financial inducement might help keep Eddie sweet. He wanted to pay the money he had brought with him from France to Freda and his daughter in the event of his death while serving his country. To another MI5 man Eddie talked about the ultimate risk ("If his betrayal of the Germans is discovered, he will pay with his life") and how valuable his continuing mission would be. Eventually, MI5 allowed him to keep the money, Laurie Marshall agreeing that an extra £350 should be added to a war bond for Eddie. (Booth, 2007, Loc. 3056)

Death was often written into the contract, whereby a sum of money would be passed to a relative, as in the case of Harry Williamson (Tate):

On 25 August 1940, Wulf Schmidt [Williamson] was informed that he would leave Hamburg the following day, to embark on his espionage mission in England. After he had performed his mission, he had been promised a good job in the colonies after the war, and 7,500 Reichmarks [*sic*]; if he should die, 10,000 Reichmarks [*sic*] would be given to his sister. (Jonason and Olsson, 2011, p. 9)

Transferring money from the employer to the agent was necessarily unconventional:

Tate made repeated requests to the Germans for more money to continue his travels around the UK. The Germans responded by saying that a friend, who was tall, blond, blue-eyed and with a wart above the right eye, who Leonhard/ Tate knew from the Phoenix Hotel in Hamburg, would at the end of April arrive with £300 and a new crystal for Tate's radio equipment. They had also been considering another plan to send him £300 by post. (Jonason and Olsson, 2011, p. 69)

In one instance, Williamson would receive his money by borrowing a copy of *The Times* (inside of which was an envelope) from a Japanese man on a bus (Jonason and Olsson, 2011). In other cases, payment was not in cash—for example, Chapman received his British payment in the form of investments in the London Co-operative Society, and a 3 percent war loan (Macintyre, 2007).

Chapman preferred his payment from the Germans in cash, but his handler, Von Gröning, opted to hold Eddie's money "in credit," thus becoming his banker:

> The Abwehr decided to award Chapman the sum of 110,000 Reichsmarks: 100,000 for his "good work in England," and an additional 10,000 for the plot to sabotage the City of Lancaster. This was some 27 per cent less than the 150,000 Reichsmarks he had been promised in the original contract, but it was still a large sum, and an accurate reflection of circumstances: the Abwehr was only about 73 per cent sure Chapman was telling the truth. Like any experienced contract-criminal, Chapman asked to be paid "in notes," but Von Gröning said that the money would be held for him "in credit" at the Oslo Abwehr headquarters, where Chapman could "draw on it when necessary." (…) He would also receive a monthly wage of 400 Kroner. Chapman signed a receipt, which was countersigned by Von Gröning …. (Macintyre, 2007, p. 231)

A limited monthly payment was also on offer to Dušan Popov (Tricycle): "A [German] representative was sent to Lisbon to inform Popov that there was no question of payment in advance for any report that he produced. The best Berlin could offer was a three-year contract with a Swiss import/export company, which would guarantee him a minimum of 1,500 Swiss francs a month" (Miller, 2004, loc. 4386).

Such innovative forms of payment had the potential to backfire—for example, when the Abwehr paid Chapman in forged British currency, the spy was at risk of being arrested for fraud (Macintyre, 2007).

REMUNERATION MUST BE SECRET

The secrecy of pay in the world of big business is not a new idea. Many employers discourage their employees from talking about their salaries, and there is a good reason for employers wanting to keep this information under wraps: "If you know you're being paid less than a colleague who's doing a very similar job, there's a chance you'll ask for higher pay."[1]

---

[1] https://www.cbc.ca/radio/sunday/the-sunday-edition-for-august-23 -2020-1.5689297/we-guard-more-secrets-about-salaries-than-about-sex-and -employers-want-to-keep-it-that-way-1.5689307, accessed February 9, 2022.

The reason why secret service organizations conceal their remuneration strategies is somewhat different—the nature of the work means that pay for it too must be hidden. A sudden injection of cash may expose the spy. Such concerns arose when Ashraf Marwan (the Angel) was recruited by Mossad. His biographer noted, "It was clear that an infusion of cash could translate into a suddenly profligate lifestyle—raising questions about whether he was selling state secrets. The Mossad had faced this problem in the past, but the amounts were always small and the agents extremely careful" (Bar-Joseph, 2017, p. 51). In Marwan's case, the amounts demanded were huge, and Marwan himself extremely careless.

Yet, expensive outgoings were often cited as necessary for performing spy operations. Williamson (Tate) milked the Germans, arguing that large sums of money would buy him a lifestyle essential for networking with rich and influential people.

> The war was now going well for Germany and they were well on their way in Russia, a victory being expected before Christmas. They wondered if Tate needed a really large sum of money! In this way he could build a larger organisation. Did he believe that, with more funds, he could recruit more people to work for him? With money he could travel around more and get closer to people who knew more secrets. They wondered how much he would possibly need a month to live such a life, of course, without risking his own safety. (Jonason and Olsson, 2011, p. 73)

Managing rewards and designing reward systems are probably the areas where the practices of secret service organizations contrast most sharply with those of standard organizations. The biographies we studied contained scant information about the market rate, grade and pay structures, pay progression, pensions, benefits, and allowances. The arbitrary nature of pay, decided ad hoc on the basis of circumstances, is at the center of spy culture.

POST-SERVICE REWARDS

Spies were rewarded for their work during their service, but the job also brought a significant post-service reward. Usually, this consisted of a new identity and a well-funded quiet life, as was the case with Oleg Gordievsky, a Soviet double agent who supplied information to MI6 from 1974 to 1985 (Macintyre, 2019). Juan Pujol García (Garbo) was generously rewarded post-service by the British:

> Garbo: "I left Great Britain in June 1945 on board a Sunderland hydroplane for the United States, accompanied by Tommy Harris, for MI5 were determined to look after GARBO right to the end. The British were always marvellous to me and, at the end of the war, MI5 gave me £15,000 as a reward for my work; they arranged for this money to be sent to Caracas through the Banco de Londres y Sud América." (García and West, 2011, p. 187)

The Germans were also generous in their post-service rewards, as Popov's case suggests:

> Popov's terms of employment [by the Abwehr] were settled. It was agreed that the Germans would continue to pay all his expenses and regular fees, conditional on his performance. In addition, the Abwehr would guarantee to protect his family in Yugoslavia and make its best efforts to release any of his friends who had been arrested. After the war, Popov would be rewarded for his services with an exclusive agency to represent the Wolff industrial conglomerate in Yugoslavia. (Miller, 2004, loc. 1470)

Some spies also received awards, such as the Iron Cross—a military decoration in Nazi Germany between 1933 and 1945—or a British order of chivalry, such as the Order of the British Empire (OBE). García was awarded the Iron Cross in 1944 for services to the German war effort, although this was normally only awarded to members of the regular armed forces. Chapman was the only British citizen to have ever received the Iron Cross, according to Macintyre (2007), whereas Williamson (Tate) had to become a German citizen:

> After working for only six weeks, Tate was recommended by Nikolaus Ritter [Chief of Air Intelligence in the Abwehr] to receive the Iron Cross second class for his valuable contributions; he was the first agent to receive this coveted award. To be able to receive this award, he was also naturalised as a German citizen. (Jonason and Olsson, 2011, p. 57)

The British did not hesitate to award García the OBE:

> When the question arose about a British decoration, an honorary award of Membership of the Order of the British Empire, no such obstacles were placed in GARBO's way. It was recommended by Tommy Harris (who was himself decorated with the CBE for his role in the GARBO case), Colonel Robertson (another CBE recipient for his war work) and the director-general of the Security Service, Sir David Petrie. (García and West, 2011, p. 166)

In recognition of his service to the British, Popov was awarded an OBE:

> The citation for his OBE was couched in the following terms: "Dušan Popov originally offered his services to the British Embassy in Belgrade at a time when his own country was neutral and the prospects of a British victory did not look favourable... His active work extended over a period of three and a half years during which time he showed courage and resourcefulness. At one time, when he was under suspicion and it was thought that his contact with the enemy would have to be discontinued, he persuaded the British authorities to allow him to take the risk of meeting the enemy with empty hands and although he was subjected to a close interrogation, he came through with flying colours... The work of this agent was invaluable to the Allied cause and the channel of communication played an important part in deceiving the enemy prior to the Normandy invasion. At all times this agent has co-operated with the British authorities to the fullest extent at great danger both to himself personally and to his relatives in Yugoslavia." (Miller, 2004, loc. 4958–4969)

If rewards were generous, sanctions, in most cases, were also impressive.

SANCTIONS

In his 2016 memoir, Cornwell described a conversation with Nick Elliott, his more experienced colleague from MI6, in which he tried to learn about what may happen to him in case things didn't work out as they should:

> Self: "So what were your sanctions if he didn't cooperate?" Elliott: "What's that, old boy?" "Your sanctions, Nick, what you could threaten him with in the extreme case. Could you have him sandbagged, for instance, and flown to London?" "Nobody wanted him in London, old boy." "Well, what about the ultimate sanction then—forgive me—could you have him killed, liquidated?" "My dear chap. One of us."
>
> "So what could you do?" "I told him, the alternative was a total cut-off. There wouldn't be an embassy, a consulate, a legation, in the whole of the Middle East that would have the first bloody thing to do with him. The business community wouldn't touch him, his journalistic career would be dead in the water. He'd have been a leper. His whole life would have been over. It never even crossed my mind he'd go to Moscow. He'd done this one thing in the past, he wanted it out of the way, so he'd got to come clean. After that we'd forget it." (le Carré, 2016, p. 180)

Indeed, if the secrecy of the service was broken, the most common sanctions were a total cutoff, imprisonment, or death, administered in an

official (court decision)—or unofficial—way. Chapman had been properly informed about it by the Germans:

> If caught, Eddie was expected to keep quiet. He agreed not to divulge any of
> the names of people he was working for or who had trained him, the chemical
> formulae they had taught him or any places that were known to him. If any
> of this information was revealed, he would be punished by death (the fact
> that execution by the British would far more likely follow was glossed over).
> (Booth, 2007, loc. 2072)

Most spies were bound by the Official Secrets Act in Britain and were
not allowed to discuss their work with anyone. This clashed with an
overwhelming desire post-service to write books about their experiences.
Chapman ran into difficulties with his British employers. Following
his termination as an agent at the end of 1953, he was able to publish
his memoirs as *The Eddie Chapman Story* in 1954, after they had been
censored by the British government. He was helped by a leading tabloid
journalist of the day, Frank Owen, who added a preface to the book:
"This is all of Eddie Chapman's story that anyone is allowed to tell. It
is only half of it: for telling the other half, Eddie was fined £50 and £35
costs at Bow Street on 29 March 1946 under the Official Secrets Act."
Booth added, "The spectre of legal action overshadowed the whole enterprise. The British authorities made it clear that any reference to Eddie's
work as a double agent would lead to another prosecution" (Booth, 2007,
loc. 5570–5578).

By the summer of 1966, Chapman could finally publish *The Real
Eddie Chapman Story*, but "the publishers still had to leave out many of
the details which had been cut from the 1954 version" (Booth, 2007, loc.
5746).

LACK OF REWARDS OR OF SANCTIONS

As the case of Swedish spy Karin Lannby illustrates, the glass ceiling was
very much a factor in secret service organizations. Lannby's financial
situation was very bad when she started working for the Swedish government agency the Defense Staff in 1939. She felt her contribution to the
work of the agency was crucial and deserved better pay, but her bosses
saw it differently. They were appalled when

> ... early on Karin decided to go above the traditional woman's role. Even if
> probably during that time one could feel that changes were underway, when

the war broke out, the male worldview was back in full scale. It is men who fight and men who create strategies and make decisions at the military head-quarters. The role of women is to keep the home front, knit socks and write letters to their boys out there. At her height, a woman could join the Women's Voluntary Defense Organization and maybe sit in an air surveillance tower. But that didn't suit Karin. She wanted a far more active and meaningful role in the big game. (Thunberg, 2009, p. 199)

Men were most likely offered awards more often, but were also free of many sanctions, for example, in relation to alcohol overconsumption (see Chapter 2).

8. Termination

Personnel management and Human Resource literatures use different terms for exit from the employment relationship in standard organizations. These terms vary depending on the legislative framework and employment practices in different countries.[1] The authors describe diverse ways of exiting from employment, but they all agree on the fact that the ways vary depending on who initiates the exit. A "voluntary termination" is when a person leaves a job of their own accord through resignation or retirement, whereas an "involuntary termination" occurs when the employee has no choice in the matter—they are fired or subjected to layoff or compulsory retirement. There are also exits resulting from life events such as death in service or poor health.

Personnel managers are obliged to collect and record information on why an employment contract was terminated; they should document the reasons for leaving or for being dismissed, which would then be used for monitoring attrition and turnover. "Attrition" refers to a situation in which an employee leaves his or her job due to life circumstances (which is seen as a healthy aspect of organizational life), whereas "turnover" describes people who quit their jobs because of poor job quality (low pay, bad working conditions), which signals an unhealthy facet of organizational life. In standard organizations, an employee's exit activates policies and procedures that need to be followed by both the organization and the exiting employee. The steps should be the same, whether the employee leaves voluntarily or involuntarily. But how does termination of employment look in the world of spies?

ACCIDENTAL DEATH

In standard organizations, an unproductive employee may be "managed out" of the organization, although handling the arrangements for releasing people through redundancy, dismissal, or retirement are said to be the

---

[1] See, e.g., Wang and Shultz (2010).

most difficult areas of personnel management. Dismissal, in particular, must be handled sensitively and in accordance with three general principles: (1) the individuals should know the standards they are assessed against, (2) be told that they are underperforming, and (3) be given an opportunity to improve (Armstrong and Taylor, 2020).

In our material we have not found much evidence of these three principles being followed. Defective recruitment is bad news for security services, as ineffectual agents must be disposed of. Double agent Juan Pujol García (Garbo) recruited three inadequate subagents, and the organization had to disengage from them. Luckily, one of the subagents resigned in November 1942 after he was caught up in a disastrous deception plan. The second received poor reports, and he also resigned. The third subagent "was obliged to contract a serious illness" as his absence could only be explained by his transfer into a hospital where he eventually died in November 1942 (García and West, 2011, p. 102).

The third example illustrates a recurring theme in several biographies: that of an—allegedly—accidental death. It is not always clear from our source material whether a particular death was suspicious or accidental. The SOE's Polish agent Krystyna Skarbek could not return to Poland after her service ended, but when she applied to join the UN's British Section, she was told, "You are not British at all. You're a foreigner with a British passport" (Stevenson, 2011, p. 314). She settled in London, taking on various jobs—as a shop assistant at Harrods, as a waitress, and as a stewardess on a cruise ship. In 1952, at the age of 37, she was stabbed to death at her London home, and a spurned suitor was convicted of her murder (ibid.). The biographer offered no comment about whether this was credible.

The exit from Mossad of Egyptian spy Ashraf Marwan (the Angel) appeared to be an amicable parting of the ways, but his death was suspicious, to say the least. Prior to his demise, Marwan's payments from Mossad had been gradually scaled down, and his diminishing importance in Israel was reflected in the decreased interest Israelis paid to his intelligence. Yet, Marwan himself was unable to let go. His biographer asked,

> Why would he continue to work for Israel for years, at considerable risk to his career and life, even after 1981, when he would leave Egypt (…)? Only one conclusion makes any sense. His role as a spy fulfilled some need, and he was reluctant to give it up. Perhaps it was the excitement and risk inherent in espionage. (Bar-Joseph, 2017, p. 266)

The new Mossad chief, Yitzhak Hofi (in charge from 1973 to 1982), decided to end the relationship, but his successor, Nahum Admoni, immediately attempted to renew the collaboration. This time it was Marwan who decided to break off contact once and for all—out of a "natural desire of an aging man to bring an end to the secret, dangerous liaison he had built with the Mossad" (Bar-Joseph, 2017, p. 287).

Following this parting of ways, Marwan's secret role was made public. In 2007, Marwan fell from a balcony of his London flat, while four of his business partners were allegedly watching this happen from a building on the other side of the street. The biographer remarked that "it is entirely possible that Her Majesty's Government had no desire at all to resolve the violent death of a high-ranking foreign citizen, which, though it took place on British soil, was far removed from British interests" (Bar-Joseph, 2017, p. 304). The biography lists three possibilities: murder by business rivals, murder by Israelis in retribution for his deception in 1973, or murder by Egyptians who wanted to avoid any revelations of secrets.

GAGGING

Practices of employment termination sometimes involve "gagging clauses," often related to financial compensation. Gagging clauses are nondisclosure agreements where neither party reveals the details of separation or the level of compensation. This measure is usually implemented to avoid damage to the organization's reputation and to prevent the airing of the company's "dirty laundry." In the world of British espionage, such gagging clauses come in the form of the Official Secrets Act and relate to matters far more serious than the organization's reputation. Second World War posters in the International Spy Museum in Washington, DC convey a warning that "Loose lips sink ships" and "Rumors cost us lives." Employees of secret service organizations have been gagged post-service, and ineffectual recruits were sometimes gagged during their service. The SOE's Vera Atkins said, "If we throw out some trainees because they don't measure up, they already know too much, so they're put into other service units, and gagged by the Official Secrets Act" (Stevenson, 2011, p. 167)

Double agent Eddie Chapman (Zigzag) signed the Official Secrets Act, but failed to anticipate what followed:

> Unaware of what was coming, he signed it, thereby stating: "I understand that any disclosure by me, whether during or after the present war, of facts relating

to the undertaking upon which I have been engaged … will be an offence punishable by imprisonment." Having gagged Chapman, MI5 then sacked him. (Macintyre, 2007, p. 305)

Macintyre suggested that Chapman's fate illustrates the way in which spies are "disposed of" despite the risks they may have undertaken for their employers. Such an exit appeared preferable to "accidental death," but it seems that many spies had difficulty in accepting it. Macintyre used harsh language to describe Chapman's separation:

> Chapman had repeatedly risked his life for the British secret services; he had provided invaluable intelligence for the Allied war effort, he had penetrated the upper echelons of the German secret service, and helped disrupt V-weapon attacks on central London; but he was also a criminal, expendable, and quite the wrong sort of person, in the eyes of many, to be hailed as a hero. This was the man MI5 would now "dispose of," if he dared to bother them again. (ibid.)

Another biographer noted the remarks of a security service officer that post-service Chapman "was living 'in fashionable places in London always in the company of beautiful women of apparent culture'" (Booth, 2007, loc. 5338). Gagging did not appear to have had a detrimental effect on his quality of life.

Many other spies became disposable following their services to the war effort. In 1945, female informers were the first victims of the peace. Here is the opinion of a Swedish woman spy:

> Persons of our kind, rank and file, with no titles, belonging nowhere, and additionally *women*—will be thrown away. There is no place for us. When the war is over, there will be no need for spies, no need for us. Swallows did their duty, swallows can go. (…) We are the war's temporary workers, and nobody will feel responsible for us when the war is over. We will be the peace's first victims. (Bergman, 2014, p. 303, transl. BC)

This opinion was supported by other Swedish authors. Jan Guillou (2019–2020) reminded the viewers of his TV series that, in 1945, the agency that employed Karin Lannby had promised her a teaching job, but this promise was not kept. In 1947, she worked at the Argentinian Embassy in Stockholm; after she was fired, she worked as a journalist in Italy, where she exposed a mafia boss and had to escape to Paris. During her time as a spy, the possibility that she might be "sleeping with the enemy" was taken seriously, so her role as a successful agent only came to light after she died in 2001.

TORTURE AND DEATH

The worst-case scenario was torture and death, and several spies whose biographies we analyzed finished their careers in this way. García and West (2011) quoted the example of German agent Johann-Nielsen Jebsen, who was tortured; when he refused to give any information, he was taken to a concentration camp and executed:

> The Germans suspected that Jebsen was working for the Allies as a double agent. The day after Jebsen had reported to SIS he went to the German embassy in Lisbon to receive his [alleged] decoration. As soon as he stepped through the door of Schreiber's office, he was knocked to the floor and interrogated. On 1 April he was bundled, unconscious, into the trunk of a limousine carrying diplomatic plates and driven straight to France, where he received an official escort for the remainder of his journey to Berlin. After a brief spell in a Wehrmacht prison, he was transferred into the custody of the Gestapo, who are believed to have executed him in the Oranienburg concentration camp on an unknown date in April 1945. (García and West, 2011, p. 128)

Macintyre (2014) cited the case of Theodore Maly, born in Austria–Hungary, a Roman Catholic priest who served as a Soviet intelligence officer during the 1920s and 1930s. He was one of the controllers of the British Soviet spies known as the Cambridge Five, but in 1937, when during Stalin's Great Purge many things changed in the Soviet Union, his past as a priest was remembered. This led to him being tortured at KGB Headquarters in Lubyanka, where he eventually confessed to spying for the Germans. He was shot in 1938. Konstantin Volkov, an agent for NKVD, the Interior Ministry of the Soviet Union, tried to defect in 1945, but was reported by Philby, tortured in Lubyanka, and then disappeared.

Philby was given political asylum by the Soviets in 1963, but the Soviet Union did not always take such good care of its agents. Matthews (2019) told the sorrowful story of Richard Sorge, who, in 1944, broke down on his sixth day in a bitterly cold Japanese prison, deprived of sleep and constantly interrogated:

> Abruptly the prisoner sprang from his chair, drew himself up to attention, threw his prison coat on the floor and began pacing up and down the cramped cell, hands in his pockets. "Indeed, I am a communist and have been doing espionage. I am defeated!" Sorge shouted. "I have never been defeated since I became an international communist. But now I am beaten by the Japanese police." He sat down again, buried his face in his hands, and wept bitterly.

(…) "I will confess everything," Sorge said finally. "If I can have a rest." (Matthews, 2019, loc. 6416)

Sorge knew all about the efforts to which Moscow had gone to rescue other agents, and even told his interrogators that he was sure his old Comintern colleagues and his employers would intervene. What he did not know, or did not consider, was that both Comintern and his office, the Fourth Department, were being disposed of. "It was only when he saw the formally dressed officials that he realised that the moment of his execution had come" (Matthews, 2019, loc. 6623). Ironically, Moscow afterward celebrated Sorge, and continues to do so now.

But the KGB's treatment of foreign spies was not exceptional: "Death was part of the game. (…) More than a dozen spies intercepted through the Bletchley Park decrypts had ended their lives on the gallows or in front of a firing squad. British intelligence was not above 'bumping off' enemy spies, to use the cheery euphemism favoured by MI6" (Macintyre, 2014, p. 72). Mossad's Egyptian spy Eli Cohen met a similar end: "He was caught in the act of spying, tortured, but didn't give any incriminating information about Israel. He was hanged in 1965" (Jewish Virtual Library, 2007).

Some agents were luckier, though.

CAREER CHANGE

Some spies opted for a voluntary career change and were allowed to do so. According to Sisman (2015), David Cornwell's (le Carré) exit from the profession was related to his success as a writer. The publicity achieved as an author was incompatible with the anonymity required of an SIS officer, but Cornwell was quite attracted to the financial rewards of writing. Allegedly, it was a note from his accountant that promoted his exit: "[le Carré] would often say that his resignation from SIS had been prompted by a cable from his accountant. He had given Hale Crosse instructions to inform him when his net worth reached £20,000; and when a cable had arrived confirming that his earnings had reached this target, he handed in his resignation" (Sisman, 2015, p. 255). Sisman claimed that Cornwell was willing to leave the Foreign Office once his novel *The Spy Who Came in from the Cold* (1963) had proved a success but had asked to be kept on for tax reasons, although Cornwell himself allegedly emphatically denied this story.

Stella Rimington, the Director General of MI5 from 1992 to 1996, combined her retirement with a change of career. She had had a permanent position at MI5 since 1969, and after her retirement was made a Dame Commander of the Order of the Bath. Her own reflections help to explain why retired intelligence officers might look for another occupation:

> As my retirement date had drawn near, I had begun to wonder how I was going to keep myself amused. I did not see myself being comfortable sitting knitting in a rocking chair after all I had seen and done. My first idea was that I might take a leaf out of the book of the Foreign Office who seemed particularly good at getting their ex-Ambassadors berths as Masters of Oxford and Cambridge colleges and try for such a post. (Rimington, 2001, p. 272)

Eventually, she became a nonexecutive director of Marks & Spencer and BG Group, and has published a number of novels.

Vincent Severski, who retired from the Polish MIA in 2007, became a writer of popular spy novels (by 2020, he had written nine books). As Severski himself observed, and numerous biographers agreed, "There are many points of contact between literature and intelligence work. Imagination, the ability to correctly assess facts, the ability to predict a situation that is associated with knowledge of the human psyche."[2]

George Tenet, the Director of Central Intelligence for the CIA from 1997 to 2004, was in 2005 accused by CIA Inspector General John Helgerson of bearing ultimate responsibility for the US intelligence community's failure to develop a plan to control al-Qaeda, which led to the terrorist attacks of September 11, 2001. However, in December 2004, President George W. Bush awarded Tenet the Presidential Medal of Freedom. Tenet then taught the Practice of Diplomacy in the Institute for the Study of Diplomacy at his former university, the Georgetown School of Foreign Service. In 2007, he published his memoir, *At the Center of the Storm: My Years at the CIA,* and in 2008, became the managing director of investment bank Allen & Company.[3] In secret and standard organizations alike, it appears the "termination" of directors stands in sharp contrast to the termination of employees.

---

[2]   https://wyborcza.pl/duzyformat/1,127290,17554015,Vincent_V__Severski _Zona_szpiega_ma_trudniej.html, accessed March 11, 2015, transl. SS.
[3]   https://en.wikipedia.org/wiki/George_Tenet, accessed January 15, 2022.

FULL RETIREMENT

The transition from intelligence work was not so smooth for everyone. Retirement from espionage can cause health problems, as observed by Severski:

> Intelligence officers hardly suffer from depression when they retire. More often after leaving the service they have the so-called withdrawal problem. The young officer slowly gets into bigger and bigger cases. Adrenaline levels begin to rise. After seven to eight years of hard work, the high level of adrenaline becomes normal. When it's lacking, a void emerges.[4]

Severski's observations about retirement resonate largely with themes in personnel management literature; the reward for years of hard work can also cause stress and anxiety when the retiree misses the meaning and purpose that came with the job and mourns the loss of "the old life." In the case of secret agents, the loss of adrenaline-inducing situations is said to be particularly hard; not even the spies who were rescued from threat and welcomed with appreciation and an attractive retirement by their employers enjoyed it very much. "Ultimately a burned-out spy is a useless spy," Hanning (2021, p. 323) concluded.

When Philby defected to Moscow in 1963, he was given a medical examination, a luxurious flat, a minder, and a salary. He was also promised that his children would be financially supported in Britain (Macintyre, 2014).

> As the Cold War raged, Philby was used as a propaganda tool by both sides. The Soviets set out to prove that he was living, in the words of one apologist, a life in Moscow of "blissful peace." In 1968, with KGB approval (and editing), he published a memoir, *My Silent War*, a blend of fact and fiction, history and disinformation, which depicted Soviet intelligence as uniformly brilliant, and himself as a hero of ideological constancy. Political voices in the West insisted that the reverse was true, and that Philby, drunken, depressed and disillusioned, was getting his just deserts for a life of betrayal and adherence to a diabolical doctrine. The truth was somewhere in between. (Macintyre, 2014, p. 284)

As many sources indicate, Philby was indeed unhappy during the early years in Russia following his defection—he drank heavily, often alone,

---

[4]   https://www.polityka.pl/tygodnikpolityka/kraj/1517024,1,rozmowa-z -bylym-agentem-polskiego-wywiadu.read, accessed June 28, 2017, transl. SS.

and suffered from chronic insomnia. Hanning reported that "Philby could not grasp that he was no longer a valued agent, but a problem, especially given the KGB's obsession with secrecy" (2021, p. 325). But his compatriots in exile tried to take care of him, and in 1970, George Blake, another ex-spy, introduced him to a woman who would become his fourth wife.

> Philby's last years were quiet, dutiful and domesticated. (…) He did odd jobs for the Soviet state, including the training of KGB recruits and helping to motivate the Soviet hockey team (…). He was awarded the Order of Lenin, which he compared to a knighthood, "one of the better ones." In return, he never criticised the system he had supported all his adult life, never acknowledged the true character of the organisation he had served, and never uttered a word of remorse. In the officially approved Soviet style, he maintained that any errors in practical communism lay not with the ideas, but with the people executing them. (Macintyre, 2014, p. 285)

Philby died in 1988, was given a grand funeral with a KGB guard of honor, and was commemorated with a Soviet postage stamp.

As for Blake, his retirement did not start so smoothly. He was treated harshly after his exposure as a Soviet agent in 1963, and unlike Philby, he was not offered immunity in exchange for a confession. He was convicted under the Official Secrets Act and sentenced to 42 years in prison. Aided by his Soviet employers, he escaped from Wormwood Scrubs prison in 1966 and settled in Moscow.

Kuper (2021), who interviewed Blake before his death in 2020, concluded that all the British spies who settled in Moscow refused to repudiate their faith in the Soviet Union. Nevertheless, they were disillusioned by the dreary, decrepit, oppressive country they had dedicated their lives to. According to Kuper, Blake adapted best of all: a fluent speaker of Russian, a man without a country of origin but with ideological convictions, he was content with his Russian wife and their dacha.

MI6 agent Nicholas Elliott retired in 1968, after almost 30 years as a spy, and confessed as follows: "Rather to my surprise I did not miss the confidential knowledge which no longer filtered through my in-tray" (Macintyre, 2014, p. 47). He joined the board of an international mining and media company based in London. It must be remembered, as mentioned earlier on, that Elliott was "not obviously cut out to be a spy" (Macintyre, 2014, p. 3). Perhaps retirement was easier for those spies who were not naturally suited to the job.

9. Personnel management in secret service organizations (compared with standard organizations)

> Veracity and mendacity are (...) of the most far-reaching significance for the relations of persons with each other. Sociological structures are most characteristically differentiated by the measure of mendacity that is operative in them. (Simmel, 1906, p. 445)

Indeed, we have noticed that secret service organizations and standard organizations differ mostly by their "measure of mendacity," but also that they have more in common than one might expect (Siebert and Czarniawska, 2018). The differences concern the degree of both veracity and mendacity, and the direction of their operations.

The similarities are many: like practically all organizations in today's world,[1] intelligence agencies imitate each other—at times directly, by sending their employees to other (friendly) agencies to learn, and often indirectly, as seen from the examples of double agents. They also learn from standard organizations, best seen in approaches to training (Chapter 5), which is closely linked to methods deployed in military service, and, judging from our material, is practically identical in all countries.

Another similarity lies in the fact that such training is very demanding, which explains the extreme skills possessed by most intelligence agents. This is coupled with the fact that the people selected for recruitment were, in most cases, highly talented (Chapter 2), evidenced by the recruiters' direct observations or the agents' elite university education.

---

[1] Maurizio Catino also noticed striking similarities between the mafias he studied. In his opinion, however, it is not an isomorphism typical of contemporary organizations (DiMaggio and Powell, 1983/1991), but "a common evolutionary and adaptive response to common problems and needs by different organizations" (2019, p. 5). This reasoning does not apply to secret service agencies.

Such selection always has the potential to be faulty, but even when it was successful, the probability that highly talented and extremely skillful persons might suffer from various psychological problems was very high (see, e.g., Karpinski et al., 2018). Thus, many of the controllers also acted as counselors (Chapter 6), and—just as in standard organizations—actual therapists and psychologists were quite often asked to help.

Another similarity, quite surprising to us, was the fact that secret service organizations—just like standard organizations—appear to be full of internal conflicts (sometimes to the point of forgetting who is their actual enemy). According to our sources, such internal conflicts took place in all countries and in all organizations—British, German, Swedish, Polish, Israeli, and US.

Maurizio Catino observed a similar situation in mafias: "Constant tension exists in these organizations: competition, disloyalty, communication breakdowns, arguments, quarrels, and other forms of disorganization are the order of the day" (2019, p. 4). This similarity can be explained by the fact that both secret service organizations and mafias can be characterized as half secret. Truly secret organizations, such as the Freemasons studied by Simmel, cannot afford internal conflicts; standard organizations constantly risk revelation of their conflicts. Secret service organizations and mafias have more conflicts than standard organizations because of their closeness demanded by secrecy, but neither closeness nor secrecy can ever be complete, and, therefore, conflicts may be revealed—when the spies' work has been declassified or when some mafia members decide to become whistleblowers. Of course, mafias eliminate their competitors in more drastic ways, such as through threats and intimidation (Catino, 2019, p. 117).

IS SPYING A PROFESSION?

A profession is a disciplined group of individuals who adhere to ethical standards and who hold themselves out as, and are accepted by the public as possessing special knowledge and skills in a widely recognised body of learning derived from research, education and training at a high level, and who are prepared to apply this knowledge and exercise these skills in the interest of others.[2]

---

[2]   https://www.professions.org.au/what-is-a-professional/, accessed June 7, 2022.

Only a few parts of this definition can be applied to the occupation we have described in this book: disciplined, yes, but also in need of being disciplined. As for the ethical standards, it depends on how and by whom they are defined. In fact, ethical philosopher Cécile Fabre (2022a) made this issue the main topic of her book *Spying Through a Glass Darkly*, where she addressed the ethics of espionage and counterintelligence. She considered both negative and positive definitions, quoting the (different) opinions of various philosophers (Kant was against spying; Hobbes was in favor). In her opinion, intelligence work can be morally wrong or morally right, depending on whether it serves a cause that is just or not: "[A]gents are sometimes morally permitted, indeed sometimes morally obliged, to pass on secret intelligence about their political community to the latter's declared enemy" (Fabre, 2020, p. 454).

Fabre's book was reviewed in the *Times Literary Supplement* by an ethics counselor at MI6 (Anonymous, 2022, May 13), where they noticed that "justification"—as understood by Fabre—is values-based, and made such values explicit:

> All three UK agencies have their own ethical frameworks, based on their values. In SIS [MI6], where the emphasis is on recruiting human sources, the guiding principles are informed consent, professional care and proportionality. This means that, first, we want those who take risks on our behalf to be as aware as possible of what these risks are, and what we can and cannot do if things go wrong; second, given that we are the more powerful party in the relationship, that we must take responsibility for conducting it in the safest way possible, using all of our creative skills and energies to keep our agents safe; third, that we must be rigorous in weighing the intelligence benefits of any agent relationship against the ethical harms that are intrinsic to it. (Anonymous, 2022, May 13)

Fabre answered this review and the letters that followed:

> … the ends served by intelligence agencies must be, as a matter of fact, morally just. Even when they are just, the political regime that claims to pursue those ends must be legitimate. Even when both conditions are met, intelligence activities that involve deceiving, manipulating, betraying and exploiting individuals, many of whom are innocent of wrongdoing, are not thereby and always morally justified. Sometimes, however, they *are* justified. (…) I do think that, at the same time as we justifiably pass moral judgement on what spies do, we also owe it to them to be mindful of the physical, moral and psychological costs that we ask them to bear on our behalf. (Fabre, 2022b, July 8)

So, is the existence of spies accepted by the public? Possibly, as a necessary cost related to security and defense, but approval is by no means guaranteed. There is no doubt that spies possess special knowledge and skills, derived from education and training at a high level, but it is unclear whether or not these originated in a widely recognized body of learning and research (is Cambridge University good for training spies?). Especially problematic, at least in the eyes of some commentators, would be their willingness "to apply this knowledge and exercise these skills in the interest of others," rather than themselves. However, as pointed out by Dent et al., "professions developed more as a means of controlling an occupation than necessarily as an altruistic service to others" (2016, p. 1).

Andrew Abbott's definition is more inclusive: "A profession was an occupational group with some special skill. Usually it was an abstract skill, one that required extensive training. It was not applied in a purely routine fashion, but required revised application case by case. In addition, professions were more or less exclusive" (1988, p. 7). In light of this definition, secret service work possesses some characteristics of the profession: spies share a knowledge system and skills, are highly trained, and restrict access to their knowledge. They usually do not form professional associations, however.

In a more recent volume, Dent et al. (2016) pointed out that professionals are usually members of a limited group, often an elite group, of a high-status service occupation. To become a professional requires high-level qualifications; professionals must pass stringent tests of competence as the entry to the group is restricted.

Therefore, what "special skill" or "competence" should spies possess? Our tentative answer is that they must be excellent imposters—that is, those who pretend to be someone else in order to deceive others.

Spies as Imposters

Woolgar et al. begin the introductory chapter to their recent study of imposters with the example of Russian agents poisoning former agent Sergei Skripal and his daughter Yulia with a Novichok nerve agent in 2018:

> ... suddenly the two suspects appeared on TV. The interviewer asked them why they were in Salisbury and if they worked for the Russian Intelligence Services to which their cryptic reply was "Do you?". When pressed about

their actual profession they offered, "If we tell you about our business, this will affect the people we work with." (2021, p. 1)

When they are asked about their profession, the suspects give the appearance of true professionals, expressing concern for their colleagues. But they are obviously imposters. The two suspects pretended to be tourists in Salisbury, although, as Woolgar et al. reminded readers, Skripal was also a former double agent pretending to be a regular immigrant, while the interviewer could as well have been a Russian propagandist posing as an inquisitive journalist.

According to Woolgar et al., in standard organizations, as soon as imposters are exposed, they are punished for their transgressions, and normality is restored. In secret service organizations, they are punished *for their exposure*, and a "return to normality" means many new efforts at imposture. The similarity lies, however, in the reaction of the general public: "The potential of imposters wherever we turn stirs a wide range of societal responses ranging from intrigue to suspicion, from outrage to horror. Suspicions about imposture, in turn, impact people's lives and social interactions. Imposters are everywhere. Imposters are trouble" (Woolgar et al., 2021, p. 3).

Our analysis of spies led us to conclusions quite in tune with the assumptions on which Woolgar et al. based their volume: imposters, professional or not, are primary motors of indeterminacy, uncertainty, and disorder in contemporary societies and, therefore, must not be seen as exceptions to normality; rather, they are a solid part of the present normality. Still, even if they are professional performers, does the occupation of spy actually count as a profession? It is the secrecy at the heart of secret service organizations that might be said to broaden the definition of professions.

Professional Closure

Professional closure is defined as a set of "social and economic devices used to limit access to a profession and prevent other groups copying, replicating or using professional skills" (Kirkpatrick and Ackroyd, 2003, p. 742). The basis for professional closure is the "definition of membership at a particular point in time, and the setting of criteria for those who may join subsequently" (Macdonald, 1985, p. 541).

The concept of closure has a great explanatory power, as it can elucidate the phenomenon of limited recruitment. Standard organizations limit the recruitment of professionals in an attempt to raise the market value of their members' work; secret service organizations do that to assert control over their numbers. Early literature on closure emphasized the role of group affiliation, including communal and associative relationships and membership in secret societies (Simmel, 1906). Later literature focused on the formal mechanisms of professional closure, which serve to create a monopoly in relation to other groups (Weeden, 2002), or professional demarcations (Suddaby et al., 2007).

Secret service work is certainly a closed profession, but not in the Weberian sense (Weber, 1933/1978), that is, they do not keep "the ineligibles" out for fear of losing their share of the market. Their closure is not motivated by concern about competition, but by the need for secrecy, as excessive openness to newcomers may cost lives. That is why spies are a closed club and why they preserve personal distance even when required to cooperate closely within the profession. The biographies of MI5 and MI6 spies in the 1950s and 1960s (Macintyre, 2014, 2019) suggest the atmosphere of complete trust within the club and distrust of anyone from outside the club. Membership of the club did not happen on the basis of licensing, educational credentials, or professional registration under statutes; it was determined by the candidate's aptitude and imposture skills.

There is more debate to be had about whether secret service work is a profession or not (Siebert and Czarniawska, forthcoming); for now, we predict that future research on secret service organizations will reveal its ongoing professionalization, signaled in Chapter 3.

HOW FAR HAVE SECRET SERVICE ORGANIZATIONS GONE ON THEIR PROFESSIONALIZATION ROUTE?

Studies of professions show that they tend to develop a common pattern, referred to as professionalization. In 1964, Harold Wilensky published a paper titled "The Professionalization of Everyone?" and noted some stages that, to him, formed a pattern: training, affiliation with university (to separate the competent from the incompetent), forming a local professional association, expanding to a national association, licensing, and finally forming a code of ethics.

Our analysis identified some elements of the process of professionalization in secret service organizations; several were held in common with other organizations and professions. One is a combination of professionalism with managerialism (Dent et al., 2016); a novelty, for example, to universities, where collegiality has been replaced by managerialism, but well known in secret service organizations, where agents were always run by others and running others. To use the term suggested by Dent et al. (2016), spies are "hybrids"—managers and professionals at the same time—by definition.

Further, whereas in standard organizations the day-to-day lives of professionals were previously mostly conditioned by what was happening in their employing organizations, at present they are more akin to secret service organizations, in which the actions of professionals—spies—are commonly conditioned by what was happening in the broader geopolitical context. Currently, in both types of organizations, the need for a more diverse workforce is driven not by organizational policies of equality and diversity, much as it may be presented this way, but by the political needs of nation-states.

There is no doubt, however, that secret service organizations include many standard organizational practices in their attempts at professionalization. Advertisements for secret service agents began to appear in the media in the 1990s,[3] in stark contrast to the "tap on the shoulder" approach practiced in the 1960s. Psychologists, as well as marketing specialists, are being increasingly employed in secret service organizations (the suspects in the Skripal case were most likely coached before their TV interview).

Greater transparency of secret service organizations is another facet of professionalization—we now know for sure not only that secret service organizations exist, but also who their bosses are. So, perhaps, could we say that the spy profession has come out of the cold?

---

[3]   See, e.g., an article by Nick Hopkins in the *Guardian*, March 2, 2017.

References

Abbott, Andrew (1988) *The system of professions: An essay on the division of expert labor.* Chicago, IL: University of Chicago Press.

Abubakar, A. Mohammed; Anasori, Elham; and Lasisis, Temitope Taiwo (2019) Physical attractiveness and managerial favoritism in the hotel industry: The light and dark side of erotic capital. *Journal of Hospitality and Tourism Management, 38,* 16–26.

Agrell, Wilhelm (2006) *Stockholm som spioncentral.* Lund: Historiska media.

Agrell, Wilhelm (2017) *Sprickor i järnridån. Svensk underrättelsetjänst 1944–1992.* Lund: Historiska media.

Anonymous (2022) Inherently despicable? Why spying agencies must prove they have a moral compass. *Times Literary Supplement,* May 13. https://www.the-tls.co.uk/articles/spying-through-a-glass-darkly-cecile-fabre-book-review/, accessed September 2, 2022.

Armstrong, Michael (2003) *A handbook of Human Resource Management practice.* London: Kogan Page.

Armstrong, Michael, and Taylor, Stephen (2020) *Armstrong's handbook of Human Resource Management practice.* London: Kogan Page.

Backscheider, Paula R. (1999) *Reflections on biography.* Oxford: Oxford University Press.

Bar-Joseph, Uri (2017) *The Angel: The Egyptian spy who saved Israel.* London: HarperCollins.

Bassett, Richard (2011) *Hitler's spy chief: The Wilhelm Canaris betrayal.* New York: Pegasus Books.

Bergman, Jan (2014) *Sekreterarklubben. C-byråns kvinnliga agenter under andra världskriget.* Stockholm: Norstedts.

Boltanski, Luc (1999) *Distant suffering: Morality, media and politics.* Cambridge: Cambridge University Press.

Boltanski, Luc (2014) *Mysteries and conspiracies: Detective stories, spy novels and the making of modern societies.* Cambridge, UK: Polity.

Booth, Nicholas (2007) *Zigzag: The incredible wartime exploits of double agent Eddie Chapman.* New York: Arcade Publishing.

Boxall, Peter, and Purcell, John (2003) *Strategy and Human Resource Management.* New York: Palgrave Macmillan.

Brockmeier, Jens (2001) From the end to the beginning: Retrospective teleology in autobiography. In: Brockmeier, Jens, and Carbaugh, Donal (eds.) *Narrative and identity: Studies in autobiography, self and culture.* Amsterdam: John Benjamins, 247–280.

Bruner, Jerome (1990) *Acts of meaning.* Cambridge, MA: Harvard University Press.

Bruner, Jerome (1995) The autobiographical process. *Current Sociology, 43(2),* 161–177.

Bruner, Jerome (2001) Self-making and world-making. In: Brockmeier, Jens, and Carbaugh, Donal (eds.), *Narrative and identity: Studies in autobiography, self and culture.* Amsterdam: John Benjamins, 25–37.

Carré, John le (1963) *The spy who came in from the cold.* London: Victor Gollancz.

Carré, John le (2016) *The pigeon tunnel: Stories from my life.* London: Penguin.

Carré, John le (2019) *Agent running in the field.* London: Penguin.

Catino, Maurizio (2019) *Mafia organizations: The visible hand of criminal enterprise.* Cambridge: Cambridge University Press.

CIPD (2021) *People Profession 2021. UK and Ireland survey report.* https:// www.cipd.co.uk/Images/people-profession-uk-ireland-2021-report-1_tcm18 -102392.pdf, accessed June 4, 2021.

Collis, Stephen (2006) *Through words of others: Susan Howe and anarcho-scholasticism.* Victoria, BC: ELS Editions.

Costas, Jana, and Grey, Christopher (2014) Bringing secrecy into the open: Towards a theorization of the social processes of organizational secrecy. *Organization Studies, 35(10),* 1423–1447.

Costas, Jana, and Grey, Christopher (2016) *Secrecy at work. The hidden architecture of organizational life.* Stanford, CA: Stanford University Press.

Czarniawska, Barbara (2004) *Narrative approaches in social sciences.* London: SAGE.

Czarniawska, Barbara (2008) Humiliation: A standard organizational product? *Critical Perspectives on Accounting, 19,* 1034–1053.

Czarniawska, Barbara, and Rhodes, Carl (2006) Strong plots: Popular culture in management practice and theory. In: Gagliardi, Pasquale, and Czarniawska, Barbara (eds.) *Management education and humanities,* Cheltenham, UK and Northampton, MA, USA: Edward Elgar Publishing, 195–218.

Dent, Mike; Bourgeault, Ivy Lynn; Denis, Jean-Louis; and Kuhlmann, Ellen (eds.) (2016) *The Routledge companion to professions and professionalism.* London: Routledge.

DiMaggio, Paul J., and Powell, Walter W. (1983/1991) The iron cage revisited: Institutional isomorphism and collective rationality. In: Powell, Walter W., and DiMaggio, Paul J. (eds.) *The new institutionalism in organizational analysis.* Chicago, IL: University of Chicago Press, 63–82.

du Bois, Jennifer (2016) MFA vs. CIA. *Lapham's Quarterly,* February 24. https:// www.laphamsquarterly.org/roundtable/mfa-vs-cia, accessed July 1, 2022.

Fabre, Cécile (2020) The morality of treason. *Law and Philosophy, 39,* 427–461.

Fabre, Cécile (2022a) *Spying through a glass darkly. The ethics of espionage and counter-intelligence.* Oxford: Oxford University Press.

Fabre, Cécile (2022b) Espionage ethics. *Times Literary Supplement,* July 8. https://www.the-tls.co.uk/articles/espionage-ethics-2/, accessed September 2, 2022.

García, Juan Pujol, and West, Nigel (2011) *Operation GARBO: The personal story of the most successful spy of World War II.* London: Biteback.

Goffman, Erving (1970) *Strategic interaction.* Oxford: Basil Blackwell.

Grey, Chris (2012) *Decoding organization: Bletchley Park, codebreaking and organization studies.* Cambridge: Cambridge University Press.

Grey, Chris, and Costas, Jana (2016) Invisible organizations: A research agenda. In: Czarniawska, Barbara (ed.) *A research agenda for management and organization studies.* Cheltenham, UK and Northampton, MA, USA: Edward Elgar Publishing, 136–146.

Guillou, Jan (2019–2020) *Agenternas världskrig.* STV-series in two episodes, filmed by Lars-Olof Lampers and Jens Aue.

Hagenbeck, Filip (2019) *Zwyczajny szpieg.* Warszawa: Wydawnictwo Czarna Owca.

Hakim, Catherine (2010) Erotic capital. *European Sociological Review, 26(5),* 499–518.

Hamidi, Ibrahim (2019) 10 factual errors committed by *The Spy* series on Eli Cohen. https://english.aawsat.com/node/1909526, accessed May 3, 2020.

Hanning, James (2021) *Love & deception: Philby in Beirut.* London: Corsair.

Holzman, Michael (2021) *Kim and Jim. Philby and Angleton: Friends and enemies in the Cold War.* London: Weidenfeld and Nicolson.

Hopkins, Nick (2017) What you really need to join MI6: Emotional intelligence and a high IQ. *The Guardian,* March 2. https://www.theguardian.com/uk-news/2017/mar/02/mi6-tells-minorities-we-need-you-why-are-you-not-thinking-about-us, accessed September 2, 2022.

Jensen, Morten Høi (2022) The fiction that dare not speak its name. https://libertiesjournal.com/articles/the-fiction-that-dare-not-speak-its-name/, accessed May 30, 2022.

Jewish Virtual Library (2007) *Eli Cohen (1924–1965).* The Pedagogic Center, The Department for Jewish Zionist Education, The Jewish Agency for Israel. https://www.jewishvirtuallibrary.org/eli-cohen, accessed July 1, 2022.

Johnson, Richard (1986–1987) What is culture studies anyway? *Social Text, 16,* 38–80.

Jonason, Tommy, and Olsson, Simon (2011) *Agent Tate: The wartime story of Harry Williamson.* Stroud, GL: Amberley Publishing.

Karpinski, Ruth I.; Kolb, Audrey M. Kinase; Tetreault, Nicole A.; and Borowski, Thomas B. (2018) High intelligence: A risk factor for psychological and physiological overexcitabilities. *Intelligence, 66,* 8–23.

Kirkpatrick, Ian, and Ackroyd, Stephen (2003) Archetype theory and the changing professional organization: A critique and an alternative, *Organization,* 10(4): 731–750.

Kuper, Simon (2021) *The happy traitor. Spies, lies, and exile in Russia: The extraordinary story of George Blake.* London: Profile.

Macdonald, Keith M. (1985) Social closure and occupational registration. *Sociology, 19(4),* 541–556.

Machado, Carmen Maria (2019) *In the dream house.* London: Serpent's Tail.

Macintyre, Ben (2007) *Agent Zigzag: The true wartime story of Eddie Chapman: Lover, betrayer, hero, spy.* New York: Crown.

Macintyre, Ben (2014) *A spy among friends: Philby and the great betrayal.* London: Bloomsbury.

Macintyre, Ben (2019) *The spy and the traitor. The greatest espionage story of the Cold War.* London: Penguin.

Madden, Patrick (2014) The "new" memoir. In: Battista, Maria D., and Wittman, Emily O. (eds.) *The Cambridge companion to autobiography.* Cambridge: Cambridge University Press, 222–236.

Marcus, Laura (2018) *Autobiography: A very short introduction.* Oxford: Oxford University Press.

Matthews, Owen (2019) *An impeccable spy: Richard Sorge, Stalin's master agent.* London: Bloomsbury.

Melman, Yossi (2019) Israel's legendary spy. *The Jerusalem Post*, September 25. https://www.jpost.com/israel-news/israels-legendary-spy-602806, accessed September 2, 2022.

Miller, Russell (2004) *Codename Tricycle: The true story of the Second World War's most extraordinary double agent.* New York: Vintage.

Palmer, Raymond (1977) *The making of a spy.* London: Aldus Books.

Parker, Martin (2016) Secret societies: Intimations of organization. *Organization Studies, 37(1)*, 99–113.

Parker, Martin (2018) Employing James Bond. *Journal of Management Inquiry, 27(2)*, 178–189.

Riley, Denise (2000) *The words of selves: Identification, solidarity, irony.* Stanford, CA: Stanford University Press.

Rimington, Stella (2001) *Open secret: The autobiography of the former Director-General of MI5.* London: Hutchinson.

Rombach, Björn, and Solli, Rolf (2019) To lead secret agents. In: Rombach, Björn, and Ek Österberg, Emma (eds.) *Leadership is the problem—and therefore not the solution.* Stockholm: Santérus Academic Press, 123–140.

Scott, Craig R. (2013) *Anonymous agencies, backstreet businesses, and covert collectives: Rethinking organizations in the 21st century.* Stanford, CA: Stanford University Press.

Severski, Vincent V. (2011–2020) https://www.polityka.pl/tygodnikpolityka/kraj/1517024,1,rozmowa-z-bylym -agentem-polskiego-wywiadu.read, accessed June 28, 2011.
https://wyborcza.pl/duzyformat/1,127290,17554015,Vincent_V__Severski_ _Zona_szpiega_ma_trudniej.html, accessed March 11, 2015.
http://kulturalnikpoznanski.blogspot.com/2015/08/czasami-zwyke-metody-sa -najlepsze.html, accessed August 30, 2015.
https://wyborcza.pl/magazyn/7,124059,20906654,vincent-v-severski-czekista-to -brzmi-dumnie-rozmowa.html, accessed October 28, 2016.

Siebert, Sabina, and Czarniawska, Barbara (forthcoming) *Where inequality is a virtue: Recruitment in secret service organizations.* A presentation at EGOS 2022 Conference, Vienna, July 6.

Siebert, Sabina, and Czarniawska, Barbara (2018) Distrust: Not only in secret service organizations. *Journal of Management Inquiry, 29(3)*, 286–298.

Simmel, Georg (1906) The sociology of secrecy and of secret societies. *American Journal of Sociology, 11*, 441–498.

Sisman, Adam (2015) *John le Carré: The biography.* New York: HarperCollins.

Snyder, Timothy (2022) *Transitions, empires, time and unfreedom.* Webinar at the University of Gothenburg, March 8. https://www.gu.se/evenemang/transitions-empires-time-and-unfreedom, accessed July 1, 2022.

Spier, Joe (2015) The saga of Eli Cohen, Israel's greatest spy. *San Diego Jewish World*, June 15. https://www.sdjewishworld.com/2015/06/15/the-saga-of-eli-cohen-israels-greatest-spy/, accessed July 1, 2022.

Stevenson, William (2011) *Spymistress: The true story of the greatest female secret agent of World War II.* New York: Arcade.

Stohl, Cynthia, and Stohl, Michael (2011) Secret agencies: The communicative constitution of clandestine organizations. *Organization Studies, 32(9)*, 1197–1215.

Suddaby, Roy; Cooper, David J.; and Greenwood, Royston (2007) Transnational regulation of professional services: Governance dynamics of field-level organizational change. *Accounting, Organizations and Society, 32(4–5)*, 333–362.

Syper-Jędrzejak, Marzena (2020) Kapitał erotyczny składową kapitału relacyjnego organizacji. In: Urbanek, Grzegorz, and Gregorczyk Sylwester (eds.) *Zarządzanie strategiczne w dobie cyfrowej gospodarki sieciowej.* Łódź: Uniwersytet Łódzki, 137–149.

Tate, Tim (2021) *The spy who was left out in the cold: The secret history of Agent Goleniewski.* London: Bantam Press.

Thunberg, Anders (2009) *Karin Lannby—Ingmar Bergman's Mata Hari.* Stockholm: Natur & Kultur.

Walters, William (2021) *State secrecy and security: Refiguring the covert imaginary.* Abingdon: Routledge.

Wang, Mo, and Shultz, Kenneth S. (2010) Employee retirement: A review and recommendations for future investigation. *Journal of Management, 36(1)*, 172–206.

Weber, Max (1933/1978) *Economy and society: An outline of interpretive sociology.* Berkeley, CA: University of California Press.

Weeden, Kim (2002) Why do some occupations pay more than others? Social closure and earnings inequality in the United States. *American Journal of Sociology, 108(1)*, 55–101.

West, Nigel (ed.) (2005a) *The Guy Liddell diaries*, Volume 1: 1939–1942. London: Routledge.

West, Nigel (ed.) (2005b) *The Guy Liddell Diaries*, Volume 2: 1942–1945. London: Routledge.

Wilensky, Harold L. (1964) The professionalization of everyone? *American Journal of Sociology, 70(29)*, 137–158.

Woolgar, Steve; Volger, Else; Moats, David; and Helgesson, Claes-Fredrick (eds.) (2021) *The imposter as social theory. Thinking with gatecrashers, cheats and charlatans.* Bristol: Bristol University Press.

Zegart, Amy B. (1999) *Flawed by design: The evolution of the CIA, JCS, and NCS.* Stanford, CA: Stanford University Press.

Zegart, Amy B., and Morell, Michael (2019) Spies, lies, and algorithms: Why US intelligence agencies must adapt or fail. *Foreign Affairs*, May/June. https://www.foreignaffairs.com/articles/2019-04-16/spies-lies-and-algorithms, accessed June 5, 2022.

Zetterberg, Hans L. (1969/2002) *Sexual life in Sweden.* New Brunswick, NJ: Transaction Publishers.

Index